I0605556

EVERYTHING IS A STORY

EVERYTHING IS A STORY

RECLAIMING THE POWER OF STORIES TO HEAL AND SHAPE OUR LIVES

KAITLIN B. CURTICE

BrazosPress
a division of Baker Publishing Group
Grand Rapids, Michigan

Published by Brazos Press
a division of Baker Publishing Group
Grand Rapids, Michigan
BrazosPress.com

Printed in the United States of America

Library of Congress Cataloging-in-Publication Data
Names: Curtice, Kaitlin B., author.
Title: Everything is a story : reclaiming the power of stories to heal and shape our lives / Kaitlin B. Curtice.
Description: Grand Rapids, Michigan : Brazos Press, a division of Baker Publishing Group, [2025]
Identifiers: LCCN 2025004905 | ISBN 9781587436635 (cloth) | ISBN 9781493452132 (ebook)
Subjects: LCSH: Psychology—Biographical methods. |
Storytelling—Psychological aspects. | Storytelling—Religious aspects.
Classification: LCC BF39.4 .C977 2025 | DDC 155.2—dc23/eng/20250321
LC record available at https://lccn.loc.gov/2025004905

Cover illustration by Soni Lopez-Chavez

Published in association with Gardner Literary, LLC, www.gardner-literary.com.

Baker Publishing Group publications use paper produced from sustainable forestry practices and postconsumer waste whenever possible.

25 26 27 28 29 30 31 7 6 5 4 3 2 1

To all the storytellers
who ground us in kinship, care, and love:
Thank you for showing us what it means to heal

CONTENTS

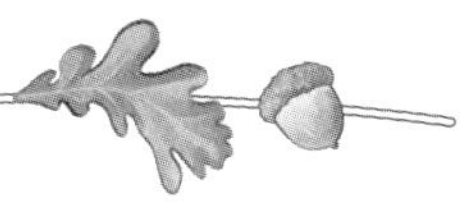

FOREWORD

Simran Jeet Singh

Not so long ago, and in a land not so far away, I heard leaders discussing religion, racism, and justice. It was a beautiful conversation: gentle yet powerful, compassionate yet difficult.

At the end of it, a woman named Kaitlin Curtice offered this wisdom: "Stay in the spiritual fire. Let it cook you."

Kaitlin attributed this aphorism to Rumi. She proceeded to explain what it meant to her and how it might serve all of us. Patience. Vulnerability. Intention. Maturation. I loved her message and found it prescient, especially given what so many in the room were struggling with, including me. Personal growth and spiritual practice are not easy. They're not for the faint of heart. It's so easy to give in, especially when the going gets rough—and it's gotten pretty rough the past few years, hasn't it?

Since hearing Kaitlin speak, when overwhelmed by the struggles of our world, I've found myself returning to her words: "Stay in the spiritual fire. Let it cook you." It's Rumi's teaching, and it's Kaitlin's too. I've made it my own, and now it's yours as well.

I've learned over the years that this is what friendship is all about. These small insights that serve us in unexpected ways, points of light that connect us with one another. The more we make these connections, the more luminous our world becomes.

Kaitlin's friendship has brought brilliance into my life, and this book on storytelling comes in that same spirit. Stories are friendships, taking us beyond ourselves and connecting us with one another. They transport us to new worlds and contexts, invoking awe and wonder, familiarity and understanding, care and empathy. As a child, I loved nothing more than encountering characters I'd never met before and developing a fondness for them. I'd root for them to prosper, with no regard for how their success might impact me. Stories made me more selfless and more compassionate. Now, I have children of my own, and I see the same in them. Stories absorb my girls for hours on end, shaping their consciousness, their worldviews, their values.

I see the power of stories in my daughters' lives, and I've studied the role stories have played in forming communities. This is why I so deeply appreciate the perspective that Kaitlin offers in this book. Stories are tools that can be leveraged for a variety of purposes, for good and for bad, to unite or to divide. It's up to us to decide what we want to do with them.

In *Everything, Everything,* Jamaican American writer Nicola Yoon lifts up the transformative potential of storytelling: "Stories help shape the way we see ourselves in the world. They help tell us who we can be and what we can achieve."[1] I see truth in her words—that because stories inform our beliefs, they have the power to change our lives and the world around us.

I also see something more. Stories don't just shape us. We also shape our stories. Realizing this has been empowering for me, particularly in a context where it often feels like our cultural narratives are being produced and circulated without our input. They're divisive and inhuman and harmful. It's exciting to realize that we have some agency, that we have a role to play. The hard part, as with so many things, is knowing where to begin.

That is the promise of this book. *Everything Is a Story* is not simply an argument for why storytelling matters (though it offers that too). It's a guide for learning how to engage a story, with purpose and urgency and care. And like any skilled teacher, this book models for us precisely what it describes. It's a story about a story, infused with Kaitlin's wisdom and generosity.

You think you write the stories
until you realize that they have
written themselves, entire
beings with entire lives you've
yet to even imagine.

They've gone on ahead
to encounter the world,
to live in it, experience it,
making their way like all of us.

And sooner or later,
those stories find their way
back to us again,
reminding us, maybe, of
who we were all along,

that we also began as a story,
grew up and grew out into the world,
only to return home to ourselves
to write our own life as we always
hoped it would be.

AS WE BEGIN

Story is the biggest, most expansive subject I could possibly write on. History is written with stories, societies rise and fall to stories, oppression is born in stories, we fall in love with stories, revolutions and movements begin with stories. *It's all about the stories.*

Stories are as magical as they are mundane; they make up the very essence of who we are as human beings. One of the things I struggle with most as a writer is this question: Am I simply writing about the same thing over and over again, using different metaphors and ideas to get the same concept across?

Perhaps. But, when I step back, that is also how stories work. Throughout time, we are repackaging many of the same stories: redemption, spirituality, power, grief and pain, ecstasy, and, yes, the magic and the mundane of humanity. Look at modern-day fantasy war stories and see Tolkien's influence stitched throughout, or how Tirzah Price brilliantly crafted murder mysteries using Jane Austen novels as a starting point, or how we retell fairy tales and myths again and again so that they can teach us something about ourselves that we may have forgotten.

This is a book of stories, but it's also more than that. This book is a way for us to ask questions *of stories* and to wonder how we use stories to harm or heal ourselves, one another, and this earth. This book is a chance for us to examine how storytelling has been a revolutionary tool for love and a weapon used for power and submission throughout the centuries.

Instead of covering all there is to say about stories, I want us to understand how stories happen. I want us to follow the life cycle of a story, from birth to maturity. I want us to understand that stories are alive, just as we are, that they are a part of us, just as we are a part of them.

This book will follow the life cycle of a story—following the life of an oak tree—which will give us space to unpack different seasons of life: seed (birth of a story), sprout (adolescence of a story), sapling (adulthood of a story), and mature tree (elderhood of a story). I conclude with a dropping seeds section (asking what the future of storytelling means for us).

In each part, each life season, we can ask what a story is doing and how the story is growing. Again, stories are alive, so we get the opportunity to ask, with great care and attention, what it means to tell a story, to be part of a story's growth.

Why the oak tree? The mighty oak is an important symbol in cultures all over the world. In Scandinavian and Celtic cultures, the acorn is a symbol of growth and power, life and fertility. It is a staple food for Indigenous peoples in the Sierra Nevada foothills and mountains, and around the globe. Acorns and oak trees are universal, tying humans to one another throughout history. The acorn is also a personal favorite relative of mine, and I can't wait for you to learn more about them.

I want to pause here to point out that throughout this book, stories will be referred to as *they/them*. Much like Mother Earth and the creatures around us, stories too are alive, moving and breathing, shaping the world that they continually encounter. Let's remember that.

Experiencing the world through words and ideas is how I, as a poet-storyteller, move and breathe, so it is my honor to try to grasp the idea and power of a story through their life and how that life actually affects human history. I'll be sharing bits and pieces of my personal stories with you; even in those personal stories, I hope to shed light on how stories shape us on an individual and collective level.

This is not a book about craft and how to write a story, though I hope that in examining the power of stories, we might ask how the stories we tell about ourselves and one another came to be. The complexity of these questions brings me to the way I've divided this book—by life seasons, by life cycles of a story, because we are, each and every one of us, encountering stories at different phases of our own lives.

A few years ago, I watched a movie with my oldest kid, and there was a moment when the two main characters got in a huge fight, the most complex, climactic moment of the movie, when things got really bad before they got better. These two characters had to fight, had to work through the most difficult stuff in order to solve the problem and get to some sort of resolution.

My child was so upset by this moment that he didn't want to finish watching the movie, but I reminded him that we *need* the conflict to get to the resolution. I told him to hold on, to wait and see. Believe me when I say, as someone who grew up constantly trying to avoid conflict, that I don't enjoy it either. I wish we could just work our way through things with tenderness in our eyes and calmness in our words, but that's not often the way things work when stories push against one another and challenge everything we hold dear.

That's why I'm writing a book about stories—because I'm a storyteller and *we are the stories we tell*. We are in a story right now, asking what comes next, grasping for a solution to the turmoil. I believe this world is in a deep, conflictual, prophetic moment, and we are asking who we are in a lot of ways, reckoning with the stories we've told, the stories we hold, and the stories we hope to pass along.

In the midst of the turmoil, I believe we can become partners to the stories that are told, that we can celebrate our role as humans who get to be part of the story. Where there are stories of hate, war, genocide, and pain, there are also stories of love, peace, belonging, and joy. I believe we can embrace the kinds of stories that propel us toward care for ourselves, one another, and Mother Earth.

May we journey together, with one another, with the stories we tell and the stories that tell us who we are, toward love, kinship, and care in this world.

PART 1

SEED

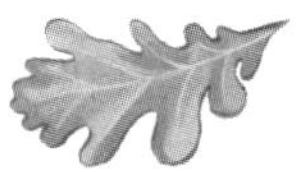

Before and beyond all struggle, what every human seeks is the peace of such joys as lovers, parents, children, and friends experience. Nothing beyond.

—William Bryant Logan,
Oak: The Frame of Civilization

The Story Is Born

It does not matter where they began—in the heat-
winded desert,
in the thick mists of a rainforest, in a quiet suburban
home,
in the depths of a city, beside roaring waters, in the wild
fold of a mountain.
Somewhere, somehow, Story is born.

They are given breath and life, and begin so small,
so small like an acorn.
You can hold them in your hand.
They are tiny, fragile, ready to grow into someone
quite mighty, and everyone around them knows it.

1

THE ORIGINS OF STORIES

Who first told you the
story of yourself?
Who decided how
you'd be raised,
where, why, and when?

Who made you think
certain things of
that holy body,
exceptional mind,
and thoughtful heart?

Who held the power to
shape your everything?

On what day did you decide
to revisit the story?

At what time did you discover
that it was all too much
and not enough?

Where were you when you
promised to love that
body, mind, and heart again?

Who helped you find
your way home to yourself?

Who gave you pen and paper
to write the story
as it always should have been?

Tell me the story again,
and we will grieve what's been lost
and rewrite the next chapter,
and the next, and the next,
and every moment that follows,
for ourselves, for each other,
and for every story
yet to be imagined.

Birth is the beginning of life, of everything that we know and understand as humans, so it makes sense that as we begin to imagine what a story actually *is*, we liken it to an acorn, seeing it as a seed, as a newly birthed being.

Five to seven months after pollination and fertilization, an acorn falls from an oak tree. Acorns lie dormant on the ground from fall to spring, so it takes time for acorns to become who they need to be, for their lives to begin and take form.[1] So it is with a story. Some may lie dormant on the ground, waiting to grow, to become, to find out who they are one day going to be.

Just as acorns are their own beings that have agency but also need the surrounding world to thrive and grow, so it is with stories. Stories are alive, taking their own presence in the world. They are nurtured, every story that grows and becomes—even those that are detrimental to us.

If you look at a group of several acorns together, you'll notice that each is different—perhaps one cap is tipped to the side like a hat on a small head, or the body of another is elongated with a sharp point at the bottom. Like acorns, stories show up in different bodies and forms, and as we get to know stories, we consider what they are capable of.

I share the following poem with you as we begin our journey together, a poem I wrote as I reflected on a special moment, years ago, that I shared with a new friend I'd met at a spiritual retreat in the desert. I offer it to you as we consider this magical reality that we are the story—the acorn, the seed being born all at once.

A friend once told me
I was a lot like an acorn
expanding beyond its bud
with effortless potential.
If an acorn is the beginning,
so is a story, and if I am an acorn,
I, too, am waiting to be told.
So, then, are you, an acorn,
growing through your beginnings
and making your way into
new phases of fullness every day,
making your way toward
the mighty oak, the elder of all elders.
We are stories, seeds, beginnings,
the blessed essence of
what it means to be human,
growing seasonally
until we find our way back

to the holy compost pile.
We are the seeds, the stories,
the changing landscapes,
the longing and hope
of all future days.

It's not often you stumble upon a place and say to yourself, *This is one of my favorite places in the whole world.* But I did, on a chilly October day in Wisconsin.

On Ho-Chunk land, next to a small body of water called Lost Lake, I sat beneath a small but mighty oak tree, who held and sheltered me for the weekend, who became a dear friend. When I first saw the lake and heard the story of the Ho-Chunk people—that this lake was nearly lost due to colonization and rapid population growth and that it was tenderly yet ferociously cared for by the sisters at Holy Wisdom Monastery in partnership with the Ho-Chunk—I was touched beyond belief. What was nearly lost was found and restored, including the prairies rising up around the lake, tall grasses and pollinators giving protection and care to all that rests around it.

I was at the monastery for a speaking event, and that evening someone had gifted me a pouch of tobacco, which I took out to the prairie the next morning, to that same oak, and used my left hand to sprinkle the tobacco that we call our medicine while my mouth and spirit prayed. *Migwetch, Segmekwe, thank you for protecting us and caring for us.* I said good morning, *mno waben,* and gave the oak a kiss on their rough bark, thanking them for being alive, for being a friend, for being a mentor and guide, an elder, my teacher.

We think sometimes that stories are born in us humans, that we create them and sustain them, that we have the power to twist and change and even destroy them. And, yes, we do, especially in those early years of our lives as we figure out who we are, but notice the stories told in the world around us. All those stories were ushered into the world at one point, making their presence known. Those origins matter—who was around, how their birth happened, what the environment was that bore them. For the Ho-Chunk people, practices like controlled cultural fires were part of their seasonal lives, practices to manage oak ecosystems and keep species safe and protected. But controlled fires are one practice among many lost to colonization over time. But what has been lost can be restored, and this oak tree friend I found at the Holy Wisdom Monastery taught me that resilience and stories are held in our very bodies from our very beginnings.

When I spent time with this oak tree, I remembered not just the tree's presence but also the collective presence of the Ho-Chunk people, the land and the water, all the creature kin of the area, and, yes, all the settlers who showed up along the way. I acknowledged the origins of kinship and even hardship that started well before my standing next to this oak. These origin stories can never truly be severed.

We may be storytellers, but we are always inheriting stories—from Segmekwe (Mother Earth), from the trees and the waters, the ants and the coneflowers, and, yes, of course, the oak trees.

Consider the story of your own birth. Who was there? What happened? What were the conditions of your coming into the world? We honor one another with birthday parties and gifts every year, but do we thoughtfully reflect on that moment when the world shifted a little, simply because we were in it?

The world also shifts with a story's birth, with a story's beginning.

Here's another question to consider: Is any story completely new and unique? Our birth stories as humans are unique to a point, but we are still human. Acorns fall to the ground and go on their own journey, but they are still acorns. So, what makes a story magical? I'd say it's the journey that a story takes—who the story encounters, how they are shaped, and where they end up.

We are told so many stories throughout our lives, stories in childhood and as adults, stories as we age into the last stages of these human-body lives. We are told stories about creation, about life and death, about family, about friends and enemies, about what we should believe. Sometimes these stories give us room to breathe and grow, and sometimes they suffocate us.

One day last year, in the late afternoon of a chilly autumn day, my oldest child and I gathered a handful of acorn bodies, and I felt the acorns speak to me, reminding me that they'd been around a while and they'd seen the whole of creation in a way that I never will.

With grace, those acorns spoke to me, and I stretched out my palm and looked at them and said yes, once again, to the great mystery that envelops me and causes me to stop breathing and to breathe again, to rest in awe of a world constantly telling me stories that point me back, again and again, to the truth of The Sacred and the sacred magic found in every corner of the universe.

I think of creation stories from cultures around the world when I hold an acorn, when I consider what exactly a story is. In the Anishinaabe and Haudenosaunee creation story, who is Skywoman, and why did she gently land on the backs of geese to come down to Earth? How did the earth become Odin's wife *and* daughter in Norse stories? Why are there multiple cycles of creation in the Aztecs' story? And how did Esege from the Mongol creation story create the earth out of void darkness?

I'm a storyteller, so every time I learn about another way that humans try to make sense of the world, I get excited. This is what we *do* as humans! We enter into stories, tell those stories, *live those stories,* and sometimes we end up chasing those stories when they take on a whole life of their own. We use stories to affirm what we already believe, and sometimes we even use stories to confuse the truth, to spread lies, and to hurt others.

The best way we honor the origins of stories is with intention and curiosity, ready to ask questions of the stories themselves, questions like, What is this story teaching me here? What does this story teach me about the way I treat others? We can use stories to ground ourselves, or we can use them to keep breathing in and out the narratives that harm us and others. The courageous life is one where we keep leaning in, where we celebrate the complexity of a story and their origins and keep sifting along the way.

So, let's settle into this moment, into this celebration of birth.

Imagine you are holding a small acorn in your hands. You are nurturing the acorn, helping them become who they are meant to be. Hold care and compassion. Take a deep breath, plant them in the dirt, and move on.

Below is a ceremony for honoring a story. If you want to go deeper into a practice beyond this book, I encourage you to spend time in this ceremony and see what you learn about the birth of stories.

Ceremony for Honoring a Story

Light a candle.

Bring an object to your space that represents a story—maybe it's a book, journal, acorn, rock, flower, or some other item. Lay it near the lit candle.

Take four deep breaths to honor the four directions.

We honor here that we are storytellers, keepers, those who pass on stories. This is not something to be taken lightly.

Pick up the item that represents a story and hold it in your hands.

Close your eyes, feeling the item, honoring the life of a story, the journey they will take and the power they will hold.

In your heart or on a journal page, commit to the well-being of the story, commit to holding and passing on stories rooted in love and kinship.

Take four deep breaths to honor the four seasons of life.

Blow out the candle.

I hope that in honoring the story, in honoring the seed, you recognize them as a kind of home within yourself, where everything begins.

When we think of a story as a living being that moves about this world, we must also consider stories as homes and homes as embodiment. In my book *Living Resistance,* I share from the wisdom of Najwa Zebian in her book *Welcome Home* about the power of stories in building homes within our bodies and lives—we can live in rooms of self-hate or rooms of self-love. Both types of rooms tell a certain story about us.[2]

If we continually choose a room of self-hate, we begin to tell stories of self-hate, stories that can get passed on from generation to generation. If we choose a room of self-love, we find a different reality, and those ripple effects emerge with tenderness and care. But it's not always as simple as this. Skywoman went on a grueling and terrifying journey before the geese caught her on their wings and gently lowered her down to her new home on *Mshike,* Turtle's back.

We are not automatically given *home*. Some of us journey to find it, and home doesn't always mean the place where we grew up, does it? Many of us are still finding home. When I'm asked where I'm from, I always stumble, because I can't really answer that. I've lived in so many places I feel like a bit of a nomad, and

I've known people from many places who welcomed me as family, as kin. A spiritual home, a genealogical home, a physical home—these things take time and examination, just like that tiny acorn we hold.

As we enter into this journey together, as we consider the origins of a story, the very seed we tenderly hold in our hands, we acknowledge what it means to look for home, to journey toward home, to find home, to create home, to sustain home. Along the way, we go beyond ourselves, asking what it means to be home to others. May we begin there.

2

OAK STORIES

When we stop to consider the utter magic of an acorn growing into a majestic oak, the very science of this miracle draws us in—that a tiny seed, a tiny being that seems so incapable of greatness, could become the giant oak tree.

The oak is mighty in more ways than one and contributes to their environment in countless ways. Oak leaves, as they fall in autumn and remain on the ground through winter, purify ground water, prevent flooding, and help creatures live in safe ecosystems. Douglas Tallamy shares in his beautiful book *The Nature of Oaks*, "Leaf shape tells us both evolutionary and ecological stories."[1] Oaks have provided wood for boats and lodging for centuries, acorns—ground into flour for sustenance and nourishment—have provided food to many Indigenous cultures worldwide, and oak trees remain a symbol of strength for many communities and nations.

Kevin Wilson writes in his book *The Way of Chai* about our interconnectedness as humans: "For the extent that we see our destinies interwoven within each other in the human family is the extent to which we can create spaces for mutual belonging and unconditional acceptance in a world that often doesn't know it needs them."[2]

This sense of belonging and interconnection reflects how oak trees have been a part of human existence for centuries, becoming a beloved and powerful symbol in cultures and religions, and a means of survival for people around the globe. Pause to consider the oak's sheer physical power—oak trees can grow to a hundred feet tall and can have a circumference of twenty feet or more.

The Wi'aaSal, an oak tree in California, has been protected by the Pechanga Band of Luiseño Indians for generations. *At least* a thousand years old, it is the oldest living oak tree in the world. The Angel Oak of South Carolina is a state treasure, believed to be around four hundred years old. The Darley Oak in Cornwall, believed to possess magical qualities, is about a thousand years old. The largest oak tree in the United Kingdom is the Major Oak; it is associated with the famous story of Robin Hood and has a girth of thirty-three feet. Some locals believe it has the largest oak trunk in the world.[3]

Expert forest maker James Godfrey-Faussett writes about the history and steadfastness of the oak tree: "The oak family has graced our planet for a remarkable 65 million years and is one of its most ancient species. This long-term survival can partly be put down to the design of acorns. The hard shell protects the seed (or to be correct, the fruit); naturally occurring high levels of tannic acid protect against fungal and insect threats."[4]

The oak is even a haven of symbiosis, sheltering and working in active relationship with all kinds of animals, lichen, and fungi.

It is no wonder the oak tree appears majestic to us humans. But you don't have to physically visit these trees to know how sacred they are—you can look in history books and scan stories throughout time, across cultures, religions, and places, to understand how incredibly important the mighty oak is to so many.

The oak tree has a deep connection with Druidic cultures, Roman and Greek mythology, Baltic cultures, Christianity, and many Indigenous peoples around the world who consider the oak tree a symbol of safety and security, of peace and gathering.

The Druids believe the oak tree is divine, and they treat oaks with respect, gathering the bark for their daily health, medicine, and rituals.

The oak tree was sacred and powerful to many, from Zeus to Thor and beyond, whose cultures recognized that the oak tree is struck by lightning more than any other species of tree and therefore holds the power of thunder and lightning.

Indigenous cultures still use acorns and acorn flour in many meals today, honoring the ancient tradition of cultivating this essential ingredient. This should cause us to pause and reflect on how Mother Earth has supplied essentials for our daily needs. In the culinary world, we are seeing a resurgence of restaurants trying to return to the sacred origins of food, and acorns play a large role in that.

The state of Michigan, which is land to the Anishinaabe people, commissioned Amber Morseau of the Pokagon Band of Potawatomi Indians to create artwork for a resource document for social studies standards. Below is how she describes the artwork for the project, featuring oak trees. As you read the description, take it in like a ritual. Read slowly and imagine the beauty of kinship and belonging shared.

> In the middle of the illustration, we have an "Auntie" offering teachings to children in her outdoor classroom by the water. She is surrounded by students offering berries to her, symbolizing that we are not just delivering knowledge to our students but we are gaining knowledge from them as well. These berries come from a bush, adorned with fire, representing the knowledge that is offered by our Tribes. . . .

> On the far left of the illustration, you will find a mighty oak tree standing tall, keeping our relatives in the center safe and guarded by the woodlands. This oak tree symbolizes the keeping of this sacred knowledge and the significance it holds to the Anishinaabe People. Teaching under this tree by the water and with the water's relatives is significant because there it acknowledges the ecosystem that exists beyond the human understanding which is always present in our teachings. This is to say that all things are relative and all things are connected.[5]

Because the oak tree is so powerful and considered so sacred, we find imagery around the world that reflects that essence, understanding through art how much oak trees, acorns, and leaves teach us about ourselves. I think of the pagan symbol the Green Man, a man with (often oak) leaves flowing around his face, sometimes with vines or flowers growing from his mouth. The Green Man can be seen in churches around the world, on street corners in architecture, in buildings from New York to London, with the earliest known examples found in Lebanon and Iraq. He is a representation of life and rebirth, the very thing stories also represent in many ways.

When I decided to write this book—embarking on a journey of learning more about the mighty, sturdy, kind, thoughtful, enduring oak as a way to understand the sturdy, enduring legacy of a story—the connection between a story's life and an oak tree's life seemed fitting, a connection that could not be easily broken. I wondered about the lessons, the myths and stories that surround the acorn, the oak tree, their resourcefulness and presence in our world today. From those lessons, may we glean wisdom and strength, and may we use this metaphor to guide our own storytelling, our own tending to the cultures, mythologies, and spaces that shape and surround us.

When I think of the power of trees, I think of Vermont, my home for eleven months in 2020 and 2021. Our beautiful and difficult short season there reminded me of the need to return to rootedness—of being grounded like a tree. And it testified to the sacred power of finding and creating home. (Portions of the following are from a journal entry I wrote about our season of living in Vermont.)

We lived in Vermont for only eleven months, but for the last two, I attended beginner tai chi classes at Long Wind Farm, a fully organic tomato farm in our small town. I didn't know what to expect when I arrived for that first session, but I knew that the ways I'd been dealing with my body, my story, my own trauma hadn't been enough over the last nine months. I was in a season of what my therapist helped me understand as ruminating, where I'd spend my mornings journaling and reading, but what I was really doing was thinking about my own trauma and story and letting those stories spin around and around in my mind until I became physically exhausted.

So when I found out about this tai chi class, I was drawn in immediately. I'd always wanted to try something like tai chi, something to ground me, something slow and steady that would cause me to pay attention to the tiny movements of my body, of my soul. We started out slowly, gaining traction on a few movements at a time, and a few weeks later when I knew we were leaving Vermont to move to Pennsylvania, I was a little bit disheartened that I was losing this momentum.

This is how it works with our bodies, our minds, our hearts, with the reality of starting over with something, some season, even someone in our lives—it takes so much time and work not to get back to where we were before but to figure out where we are going.

This is where the power of story comes in: What are we saying to ourselves about the season we've left behind, and what are we saying about the season we've stepped into, the one we are daily trying to create and sustain with any level of health or care?

Most of the time, we probably aren't paying attention to these questions. We're just living our lives, and life is just moving us along in whatever direction it chooses. Maybe the story is just writing themselves and we have no control over the narrative. But what if we did?

One day, we gathered on the large concrete parking lot overlooking the river to hold class as a storm approached. The wind picked up halfway through. There were some concerned looks, but we kept our practice going, movement by movement, an eye on the distance, our feet planted firmly against the ground beneath us.

Our teacher would pause to remind us again and again to steady ourselves, to imagine our bodies like the trunk of a tree, our roots going deep, drinking in water from the soil, holding steady in times of trouble, remaining planted no matter what comes our way. So, move by move, I'd hold that image of a tree, trying to summon the courage to remain steady, trying to trust my body to do what it needed to do to remain tethered, grounded, just like the oak.

This is probably what I learned most from my tai chi class: how to plant my feet and trust them, how to let my whole body lean into the reality that I am solid, I am steady, I can hold firm when everything around me feels like it's crumbling.

We left Vermont soon after I started the class, and I grieved as I said goodbye. Where in the world would I ever again find a tai chi class that meets by a flowing river on an organic tomato farm that's been there since the '80s? I wouldn't, and I knew that. But I was taking the lessons of embodiment with me, and that was absolutely enough.

This, too, is what a story does, stories of faith or stories from our ancestors, stories passed down from generation to generation or the powerful stories we read in books or experience through poetry and other forms of art: A story grounds us and reminds us that we are okay, that we are steady in an unsteady world. Stories keep us going when we don't know how. Stories get us out of our rumination patterns and ask us to imagine the world anew. Stories give us the courage to enroll in a tai chi class on an organic tomato farm with a group of strangers just to see what kind of magic is waiting on the riverbank, to see how deep our roots can truly go.

And when we decide to find out, we find ourselves. And the stories told there become the seeds that birth the world around us.

Indeed, we find ourselves ushered into a world waiting to give birth to stories that shelter and hold us.

3

STORIES ARE MIRRORS

We often judge ourselves against others. I did the same when I was young, often comparing myself to friends (even before social media), and sometimes mirrors were a painful reminder of the stories I told myself about myself. When I looked in a mirror, I was detached from the young woman I saw, because in many ways, I was detached from my own body, retelling the stories I'd been told in other ways—that the body is evil and the spirit is the real focus, that being Indigenous is something to assimilate away from, that being a girl is a constant test of purity.

Growing up Southern Baptist, I was told not to drink (or dance or have sex or dress in clothes that were tempting), so I was always wary and judgmental of people who did. And on top of that, as an Indigenous person, I was also told (by non-Native people), "Indians shouldn't drink because you will probably all become alcoholics."

Based on these collective narratives and stories, I believed something about myself and about the world. For many years, it was difficult to distinguish between who I was and who I was *told I was.*

Our stories are mirrors. They can reveal the ways society shapes us from childhood and what we carry from that. And, when used in the right way, these stories can lead us to tenderness and curiosity rather than judgment.

In 2019, I attended a retreat where my friend Richard Rohr led us through a mirroring ritual. He gave us a necklace, made from a thin red string and a small circle pendant, completely mirrored. In its center was the all-seeing eye, a symbol of clairvoyance and a gateway to our inner selves (and, I'd argue, our truest stories). Around the edges of the mirror pendant were the words "Our unveiled gaze receives and reflects the brightness of God," based on 2 Corinthians 3:18, a Scripture passage found in the New Testament of the Christian Bible.

We are meant to go out to the world and, somehow, learn the work and embodiment of reciprocity, in which we see sacredness and we also accept it. We give and we take in. We inhale and exhale a story of connection and care.

That's what we did that day. Richard sent us outside to connect not just with ourselves but also with Segmekwe, Mother Earth, with the lands we resided on, with our creature kin.

I recently found the journal from that day, and here is what I wrote:

What if the trees want us to know that they are survivors?
Rocks are historians?
Clouds are shelterers and dreamers?
Hills are believers?
Mountains are transcenders?
Grasshoppers are dancers?
Ants are teachers?
And we all hold the essence of one another.

That day, I found something I haven't let go of, a part of the story I wasn't often told in the kind of Christianity I grew up within as a young Indigenous woman—that I can find my sacredness, my holy story, in the story of collective belonging with the world around me, and that knowledge and embodiment are transformational.

I think about *viriditas*, the greening truth that Hildegard of Bingen wrote about and embodied in her life: The earth reflects back to us all the truth, life, and abundance we need.[1] When I found out about another person in history, especially a woman, who held and celebrated this truth that the natural world is always mirroring stories to us, I was encouraged to continue my own journey, to embrace the beauty of *viriditas* with Mother Earth.

Later, in another journal from another season of life, I wrote,

> *I want to be named by the wild things, to find my voice in their own surrender. I want to know Love as the great adventure of letting out and letting go, only to let in everything that is sacred.*

Those words, written later in my adult life, are so different from the kinds of things I wrote about myself *to myself* as a younger woman, looking in mirrors and retelling a story of sexism, colonialism, and patriarchy. To be honest, I still struggle with my own reflection, with the stories I take in and tell about my body, my heart, my voice. Stories of judgment will always harm us, but we are more than the sum of them.

It's important to pay attention to this work of mirroring, not just for our own selves but for one another. Again, stories are about community and connection, and the narratives formed around us become the narratives formed *within* us, shaping us from an early age, from our beginnings.

Let's pause and consider what happens when a story is told.

One scenario: Your aunt, who is grieving a lost relationship, is sitting with you when she receives a distressing text message. She sighs and says, "Don't ever fall in love. It's all a sham." Again and again, from an early age, you hear this message that love isn't real, that there aren't humans out there to be trusted. The story takes shape, and whether you choose to believe it or not, that story has entered into you, into the air, taking shape itself within the family, within the larger narrative. Grief bore a story, and it grew in your life and in the lives of those around you.

Or maybe it goes like this: You were born into a family that is, from an outside perspective, thriving on many levels. Your physical needs are met, you can laugh and play and have fun, but there's something missing, an element of connectedness. You grow up thinking that maybe something is wrong with you. Why can't you be grateful for this family that raised you, where you had most of what you needed but found you couldn't truly express yourself? You begin to tell a story, to live a story, that you are a bad sibling, ungrateful child, disposable friend who is incapable of connection, when truly you were noticing what was going on, the ways that physical needs were being met while needs of love and belonging were not. Maybe you were just paying attention to how this story of disconnection was passed down to you, and in listening to your own soul, you sensed the invitation to reckon with this story, this narrative.

Here's another: You were born into a family that travels a lot, and you've been to places all over the world. Sometimes you feel a little unsettled, like you want to ground yourself somewhere, but at the same time, you feel immensely connected to the stories you've heard from around the world, in cultures you'd never have known about had this not been your life. Your story is to hold the balance between gratitude and longing, letting the question *What does home mean?* live right at the center of your heart, with all the joy of knowing how beautiful the world can truly be.

Do you see how easily stories find us, how magically we find them? Whether through joy, grief, liminal space, gaslighting and trauma, or community in all its forms, we are born into the stories shared with us. We are the acorns, the seeds, that grow, just as the story does.

In 2023, I released the first of four books in my children's book series called An Indigenous Celebration of Nature. The first book, *Winter's Gifts,* features a little girl named Dani and her personal and familial relationship to the changing of the seasons and to Segmekwe, Mother Earth.

Then, in May 2024, the second book, *Summer's Magic,* was released, a story about Dani's little brother, Bo, and his love of summer and Mother Earth. In the spring of 2025, *Spring's Miracles* came out, about spring, our Anishinaabe new year, and Dani's journey of finding bravery as she goes climbing outside with her family. It was such an honor to write these stories, and every time I have the opportunity to visit a school or talk to kids about the series, I think about how important it is for them to be exposed to different stories.

At the first reading for *Summer's Magic,* I was sharing with a group of third and fourth graders about Bo, about why his braided hair is especially sacred to him (and in our Anishinaabe culture) and why his relationship to Mother Earth matters. After I read the book, a young Black girl, who also had braided hair, asked, "Is that true, about the braid?" I smiled at her and said yes, our braids can represent our mind, body, and spirit and our connection to the earth. She smiled and tenderly touched her own braid, and I reminded the kids that in cultures all over the world, people honor their hair, their braids, their ways of connecting to the earth.

I have moments like this with kids all the time at my events, because kids *get it.* They take in my story, the story of an Indigenous woman who is a writer and poet and public speaker, and they take in the stories of Bo and Dani, always asking me, "Is this real? Is this story true?" I share with them that these stories are a mix of my upbringing, raising my own Potawatomi kids, and hoping that parts of the story connect with everyone, no matter where they're from or who they are. The work of storytelling is about holding up that mirror, offering and accepting belonging.

Part of our complex journey as humans, especially as kids, is figuring out what's true and what isn't, what story to believe and what story to dismiss. We are constantly sifting through information, emotions, and experiences to figure out what's worth keeping and what should be discarded. In those tender, young years, kids are carefully exploring, trying to understand, trying to connect dots and make sense of things, and I've found that when you gather a room full of kids from all sorts of backgrounds—religious, racial, ethnic, cultural—they want to find those connections. Talking about a celebration over a big meal to honor the changing of the seasons or how we can practice caring for the earth is a perfect way to open up a whole new world of care and honesty, and I'm honored I get to guide them through that in their families and classrooms.

Stories are the mirror; they are the portal. They teach us to be honest about what we notice around and within us. As we journey deeper, as we watch stories grow like sprouting acorns, tend to them, ask which stories are healing and which are harming, we are doing the incredibly sacred work of being human. Now, we just have to ask what kinds of stories we're dealing with.

4

THE SHAPE OF STORIES

At the core of who we are as humans is a tendency to pause when life gets hard, when the world feels heavy, when things are going badly or don't seem to make much sense. We pause, and we ask questions:

- Is there a god?
- Do the powerful always win?
- Why can't I get over this?
- Why does it hurt so much?
- Who will help us?
- Am I on the wrong side?
- Are my beliefs valid?
- Did I do something to deserve this?
- Why doesn't anyone understand?
- Will the world ever get better?
- Are humans ultimately just selfish?
- Where is the love?

This is a natural response to being human, and I'd be worried if we never asked questions, because that would mean we aren't paying attention to what's happening in and around us. Our questions bring us to the stories we've been told, the ones we're telling, the ones we hope to tell. Let's try to make sense of the types of stories that are out there in the world by comparing them to the shapes of acorns.

Acorns generally come in two distinct shapes:

1. spherical (like a ball)
2. fusiform (like a football)

The shape of an acorn affects their experience in the world once they fall from the oak tree. For instance, spherical acorns are more easily picked up by animals like squirrels and deer, while fusiform acorns are easier for birds to carry in their beaks.[1]

I want us to think of stories in much the same way, in two distinct shapes that affect their path on this earth:

1. cyclical (like spherical acorns)
2. linear (like fusiform acorns)

On a large scale, especially when we look at the way history works, many stories are cyclical. Even if a story involves a character's growth, I'd say that in the end, perhaps the character is just journeying back home to themselves, to who they have always been. Though labyrinthine, cyclical journeys are common.

Other stories are linear. Linear stories tell how a series of events unfolded and follow the standard sequence: exposition, rising action, climax, falling action, resolution. I remember in school how excited I was to learn about this, to understand the way a story might take shape, how to follow the details to understand what went wrong, where, and how the problem is solved.

When I gave birth to my kids, the most difficult moment was the climax—also called the transition—the moment when labor is incredibly painful right before things start heading toward the birth itself and the baby shows up in the world. As I gave birth to my kids, I thought about stories, these stories I'd tell for their entire lives, the ones that I'd remember. When my body hurt the most, that meant I was close to the resolution, to the moment they would show up to meet us. In a story, the climax, the crux, is the peak, the hard part that we have to go through to get to the other side. It's beautiful, isn't it, and tender as well when we realize that our children are out in the world and will never be back in the womb again? Stories can indeed be linear and lead us out into the world that is waiting to meet us.

Cyclical stories involve elements like seasons, natural cycles, returning to former selves or spaces, while linear stories (those that follow Aristotle's idea of the beginning, middle, and end) focus on getting from point A to point B, or finding answers to questions by following a conflict and resolution framework.

I think of cyclical stories as focused more inward, a loop repeating in us that will teach us something about ourselves. I think of linear stories as focused more outward, a journey we are taking along a path to a destination, once again to learn something about ourselves and the world along the way.

I want you to imagine yourself as the story*teller*. Embrace this identity. The story is already alive, has already been born, is already the acorn, shaped like a sphere or a football. The story is already doing their thing in the world, as tiny as they are. You are simply the one guiding them.

Maybe you're like the bird with the fusiform acorn in your beak, or you're like the squirrel placing a spherical acorn safely in the hollow of a beloved tree. Whichever you are, tend to the story as you would an acorn. You are helping the story grow, helping them find their way in the world, for better or for worse.

Are you fostering linear or cyclical stories? Maybe a bit of both? In the past, what kinds of stories did you tend to and care for, and why? What drew you to those stories?

Even though I grew up Potawatomi, a culture rooted in cyclical stories, I also grew up in a household that followed a more linear, Western mindset. My relationship with God growing up was linear and transactional too. Do this, get that; have a question, get the answer; move on to the next item on the to-do list. I wasn't taught to honor the seasons and cycles of the earth or of my life, nor did I have patience for myself as I learned and relearned lessons. Don't even get me started on how little I knew about my own sacred menstrual cycle and the seasons I follow in my literal body, every month of the year.

Now in my thirties, I am embracing the cyclical stories. I'm living into the kinds of stories that are labyrinthine, trying my best to expand beyond linear thinking, trying to step back and honor the seasons around me and in me. If you follow any of my work, you know how much I love cycles. I love the seasons, I love paying attention to the natural world around us, I love asking what cycles I'm in and what care looks like within those cycles.

We honor the linear as well, noticing where it might be important to follow the line of something instead of the circle of it. It's a balance we hold, honoring the linear while also acknowledging that we need more cyclical rhythms in our lives.

It's also important to think about the cycles we want *to break*, the ones that keep us trapped in trauma or pain, the cycles we shouldn't repeat, the stories that shouldn't be told again and again. Maybe we can step in to break those cycles, to move from a cyclical story to a linear one, like we move from birth to a whole new life. Even though the stories have a power of their own, we get to be in relationship with them. That means we can stop the cycles from repeating and choose a new way forward.

So, let's be open to what stories are showing up, and to *how* they are showing up. If you realize that you're in the climax (or transition) of your linear story, the crux, the hard part, waiting to see what's on the other side, honor that. If you're in a cyclical story that is healthy and repeating itself, even if you don't have all the answers, honor that too.

There are a few other ways we might look at stories as we try to get a sense of what kinds of stories we're in relationship with. Consider these three types of stories as a helpful guide, a way to classify stories:

1. liminal (gray space, in between, back and forth)
2. loving (accepting, holding space, belonging)
3. lethal (oppression, cause and effect, war)

Liminal stories are the ones we cannot quite make sense of, or cannot make sense of *yet*. They are unfinished, in the making, or confusing at times. They require work to examine and understand.

Loving stories are just what they sound like—stories that affirm our sacredness and our humanity, stories that remind us of the connection we have to one another and to Mother Earth. These stories make us feel warm and fulfilled, reminding us that we are not alone.

At their worst, stories can be lethal. These are the stories that follow the paths of human or world suffering, the paths of war, the paths of death without considering those cycles of healing in and around us. I think of our incarceration systems that often don't uphold human rights, systems that foster abuse and death. I think of how we use war to commit genocide and acts of hate so vile we can barely talk about them.

When you encounter stories, ask where they fall, and remember that the life of a story is complex; stories can embody more than one space, can move sometimes between being lethal, liminal, and loving. Is a story you're encountering incredibly lethal? Pay attention to what you notice.

Every time you read a story in this book or experience a story out in the world, I want you to determine whether the story is cyclical or linear. And next, is the story liminal, meaning complex, confusing, or forcing you to ask deep questions? Is the story loving, meaning we celebrate why being human is so beautiful? Or is the story lethal, meaning about oppression, hate, and fear? Then consider how you would classify those stories.

I wonder, then, what types of stories you might come up with? What stories have shown themselves in your life? What are the shapes of your own stories, how have they changed you, and how do they continue to change you?

A.J. Eversole, a Cherokee children's book author, wrote an essay about cyclical stories, how many of our stories have been assimilated into Western storytelling, and what it might mean to honor every part of the work of Indigenous storytelling. She writes:

> We are finally seeing the support for Black, Indigenous, and people of color's stories in the world. These things give Natives hesitant hope and open our willingness to share what is ours with the world. . . . Read, share, and support the unorthodox pacing and characterization of Native storytelling structure with a passion. I truly believe the future of storytelling lies outside the western perspective and structure, and it is rich. Supporting any alternate format brings us closer to making it more mainstream and establishing its rightful place in the world.[2]

It is powerful to want to tell a better story. In fact, it's essential to being a human. Our dreams are so interwoven with our stories that often we cannot deny the stories we want to be true. I think of the book *We Are Still Here: Afghan Women on Courage, Freedom, and the Fight to Be Heard*—a collection of essays from Afghan women, all sharing their dreams of a future Afghanistan where they are respected and cared for by society. Sadly, the same year the book was published, 2021, the Taliban took over Afghanistan, resulting in ongoing human rights abuses, especially toward women and girls, depriving them of their rights to things like health care and education.[3] Women's rights continue to be stifled amid protest and public reports, and we are witnessing what lethal stories can do in the world.

Why am I sharing about Afghan women in a chapter about types of stories? Because I want to remind us that *all types of stories are human stories*. The whole point of this book is to understand that we can create stories; perpetuate stories; reframe, reimagine, and reform stories; believe stories; and, yes, sometimes let stories turn to compost so new ones can be born. And these stories of women in Afghanistan are powerful—they are complex stories and crucial dreams coming together to ask what the future might hold.

We remember that our stories are shaped by our individual experiences and also our collective experiences. And as our stories take shape, we get to be in relationship with them, to ask them questions, to consider who they are becoming, and sometimes to step in and help shape them along the way. This is a powerful kind of relationship, and we should consider it with care, because whether we like it or not, the story will keep growing.

Some days, I write stories
from bed, blankets piled
up around me, a candle
lit to keep me company,
the light still off but
the lamp still on.

Some days, comfort beats
my sense of urgency, or

maybe it's just that some
stories are meant to be
born in the dark, tender
places that no one sees.

On other days, perhaps,
the story is born in a
coffee shop, in the desert,
beside a river or with
the hum of background noise.

Wherever, however, the story
finds their place in the
anxious and weary world,
their place among the
others born in quiet
bedrooms and open fields,
where every word waits
to be sacredly, sweetly
discovered.

PART 2

SPROUT

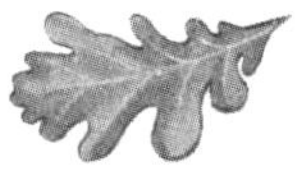

In North America, trees are our deepest connection to history, our versions of cathedrals and standing ruins.

—Lyndsie Bourgon, *Tree Thieves*

The Story Grows

Story grows up in good soil, with enough light and love to
figure out what it means to be kind, to practice kinship.
Story knows that as they grow they'll need community
and a sense of home, a sense of place.
They understand belonging.
Story has lovely family meals around the table,
with adults and elders, with wisdom and care,
where ideas are exchanged without judgment
and a diversity of voices are heard.
Story loves the practices of mealship and community
and knows that this is a special kind of life.

5

GATHERING STORIES

If we think of the sprouted oak, the seedling, as being in the adolescent time of life, we know they are just getting started. So, too, is the story, growing through adolescence, just getting started, exploring and learning who they are.

When I studied social work in college, we talked about the micro, mezzo, and macro approaches to care and service. Inspired by this system, I will focus on these ideas to guide us deeper through the life of a story. For now, let's focus on the micro—the close-knit family unit in which a story is formed and gathered.

I started watching *Stranger Things* with my twelve-year-old in early 2024. The opening scene—in which four best friends are gathered around a table in their '80s basement playing Dungeons & Dragons—produced the biggest smile on my preteen's face, because he'd been listening to Dungeons & Dragons podcasts, reading books, researching monsters and other creatures that mimic the ones he writes about in his own books, but he'd yet to see his fantasy world depicted on the screen in this way.

Dungeons & Dragons originated as a game in Wisconsin in the 1970s and has grown in popularity since, among people of many ages and locations. It is magic and history, storytelling and live-action imagination. The Dungeons & Dragons community is a tight-knit group of people who gather at their dining room tables, at communal game shops, and in library basements, all for the sake of connecting over stories.

Remember, stories are *alive*—they take shape and form. So here I witness my preteen's story sprouting and becoming—being formed and gathered at home while he listens to that podcast at our dining room table, and again at the climbing gym where he gathers at another table to play Dungeons & Dragons with his friends, and again while he watches the opening scene of *Stranger Things* in which four best friends gather around a table to grow their own stories together.

We find our way in adolescence by the stories we grow up with and by our own intuition. It's the time when we begin asking some big questions and thinking critically (if we are given the space). In the life of a story, adolescence is the time when the story's development takes shape, transforms, comes with deep presence and challenges.

In 2023, my kids and I watched *Speed Cubers*, a movie about two young men who become close friends in the ultracompetitive world of Rubik's Cube speed solving. Rubik's Cube speed solving, like Dungeons & Dragons, brings people together. It's all stories, right? The story of pushing ourselves, of discovering friendships in unlikely places, of finding solutions and the courage to face the odds stacked against us.

These stories begin around the kitchen table, with our families and friends, with the people who "get us." At a retreat, once, we were talking about family dinners. We shared that some of us never really ate at the tables in our homes; we took the food back to our rooms or sat in silence in front of the television. For others, the table was a triggering and traumatic space, where kids endured verbal abuse by parents who were not willing to listen to them. Some felt like the table was a safe place, and others felt like the table was a prison, yet both of those beginning stories shaped our own stories down the road.

Our stories first get labels in family: what kind of parent we are, what kind of kid we are, what our personality is perceived to be. I was a pastor's kid in the second half of my adolescence, and I played hard into the role of extroverted leader when, in fact, I naturally lean more introverted. Growing up, I was labeled a social butterfly, someone who'd always be there to talk with others and lead the space, yet group gatherings exhausted me and left me wanting to get back to my bedroom, shut the door, and be alone for a while to recover.

How funny that I didn't really connect all these dots until, as an adult, I had to stop performing and really ask, "Who am I?" and "What is my story?" Sometimes the stories in our lives carry far more power than we realize, and we begin to understand their power only later, when we challenge them.

In adolescence, we also begin to ask what it means to thrive or fail, to do well in life or to be someone who will never be enough. We know many of these narratives begin with family, don't they? They begin with our family circumstances, what happens in our homes, and how we are raised. Climber Tommy Caldwell writes beautifully about the journey of understanding success and fear of failure in his book *The Push*, in which he chronicles his childhood, climbing with his father, and how he became a climber in his own right as an adult. He writes about failure: "Trying your hardest and coming up short can be psychologically and emotionally exhausting. But each time it happens and you begin anew you become better, inured to the feeling. In more recent years, failure has fostered in me a deep curiosity about the mysteries I have still to unlock."[1]

Tommy was the first person to make free ascents of several major routes on El Capitan in Yosemite National Park, among other successes; along the way, he reckoned with his own stories from childhood. In facing failure, he was acknowledging the stories he'd told himself since childhood, acknowledging the complex relationship he had with his father, who was a bodybuilder and outdoor adventurer. Tommy's story is like many of our stories—even as adults, we are processing the stories told to us as kids, and our fear of failure can either push us toward some goal on the horizon or cause us to stumble, unable to look the story in the eyes at all. In adolescence, we are sprouting, growing, just as the story grows, and that means we are coming to terms with the fear and the dreams shaping us.

I have an adult version of the Frog and Toad books, written as a parody of the original, with incredible lessons, mostly about adulting and the way we reframe stories for ourselves. In one story called "Smiling," Toad struggles with people-pleasing, and at the end of the story, Frog and Toad come to a conclusion.

> "I thought you did not need everyone to like you anymore," said Frog, exasperated.
>
> "I do not need it," said Toad. "But I want it very much."[2]

Every story in the book is both laugh-out-loud funny and thoughtful, and speaks to the conundrum we find ourselves in from adolescence through adulthood: How can we possibly reframe the stories that we tell about ourselves? We can do it with people we trust who can, again, show us who we are. It's good to know that Frog and Toad struggle too and find their way together.

Rainesford Stauffer writes in *All the Gold Stars* that ambition should be aimed more toward our connections with one another than toward our accomplishments and the list of things we've done in our lives. But it begins early, doesn't it? The pressure to do well, to succeed, to check off the boxes of accomplishments we've completed. And if we don't "do well," a different story is written, usually by us and *to us*, a long list of journal entries about how we just weren't good enough.

You are the kid who makes good grades, the nerd, the stupid one, the class clown, the jock—whoever you are, often those labels end up fueling the fires of being bullied or, in other cases, bullying. Stauffer writes, "Ambition is a constellation of influences, forces that take shape before we've had a chance to define it for ourselves—sometimes before we've had a chance to define *us* for ourselves."[3]

I think of a song in *High School Musical* when all the kids sing about secretly wanting to break away from the expectations created for (and sometimes by) them. A star on the basketball team is also secretly a baker (much like my oldest, who is on the climbing team at our gym and also bakes). A young scientist also loves dancing. In true Disney fashion, they find some freedom in breaking away from the labels and expectations placed on them. Stories are incredibly powerful, and the places where we gather to tell them for better or worse—such as a high school lunchroom—become important because of what's spoken there. When I think about the gathering places that bring us to stories and bring stories to us, I of course think about libraries.

When I was little, I lived in New Mexico, and I have a very vivid memory of hanging out in the Los Alamos public library, on the tall, narrow staircase of the children's section, looking at books. My brother, sister, and I would go there after school while we waited for my mom to finish work. I could look out a small window carved into the wall, like the window of a castle, and see my older brother, Tyler, checking out the science fiction section. I felt safe and held on that staircase.

Now that I'm a parent, libraries have been a constant for us. They have also been a place to hold my deepest emotions, my gratitude for words and visions, and my tears as we've transitioned to new libraries, joined new communities, found new spaces of belonging, new spaces for stories.

Libraries mark a passing of time. They hold memories not just in their walls but in all the books we've touched and shared over the years. Libraries hold stories, thousands of them, and in those stories, we find ourselves. Libraries are incredible resources not just for communities but for families, in the actual growth and development of kids and adolescents alike. Libraries are micro spaces for us to gather, to show up with the special people in our lives, a whole world unto ourselves where we figure out who we are.

When my kids were just babies, we started going to the public library in Fayetteville, Arkansas, an award-winning facility with games, puzzles, stellar story times, an array of computers, and seemingly unending shelves of children's books. It was our haven for the four years we lived there.

I mourned deeply when we left, when we moved to a new city with a different library experience.

Then we spent about three years without a library. We moved across the country to the northeast, wrestled through a pandemic, and struggled with burnout that kept us from books and shelves, those stories and words arriving only by Amazon packages to our doorstep and visits to local bookshops when possible. There was no browsing, no quiet moments huddled on the floor with a pile of books. We ached for those moments.

In 2023, we moved to a neighborhood with a library up the road. We knew it would be a small yet mighty place, but I wasn't expecting the grief to follow me again, to sweep in unannounced. The kids, then ten and twelve, went straight to the graphic novels, young adult literature, and chapter books, and I sat down in the middle of the picture books wiping my tears away.

There is no returning in the way we think there will be. There is no going backward to my children as toddlers gathered on my lap to read a book. This is always, always the tricky thing about time. But recently, as I was getting out the Halloween decorations from the basement, I pulled out the same kids' books we've had for years—*Creepy Carrots!* and *The Berenstain Bears and the Ghost of the Forest* and *Arthur's Halloween* and *Trick or Treat, Smell My Feet.* The next morning, I found my eleven-year-old looking through them, because they hold memories, time, experiences, and stories. Those books will always be a part of us, and when I circle back to our library next week with my kids, I'll see the children's books differently, marveling at how even I have come to cherish and treasure them for what they've taught me along the way.

Libraries are scenes of power, showing who has voice in a community. Maybe we find ourselves at our monthly library book club meeting, where we are challenged to think and understand the world differently, or at a tutoring session in a quiet room. Either way, libraries can hold space for us to show up.

The root word for library, the Latin *liber*, refers to the inner bark of trees, to the paper made by those trees, to the books made by those pages and pages of paper, and finally to the places that hold those books—the libraries themselves. Oak galls, which are small growths that form on oak trees due to wasps or other insects, were historically one of the best ways to get ink from the tannins in the galls, an essential tool for the author, the transcriber. I picture a monk in a scriptorium, copying and copying words in perfect calligraphy with colored inks for a manuscript that will be read many times over. When we pause to think of the origins of something as simple as a book, even this book that you're holding and reading right now, it's pretty incredible to consider how far we've come.

Just as pages create a book, so, too, an acorn creates a tree, the stories creating narrative after narrative, living and breathing in the world.

6

STORIES OF FAITH AND RELIGION

In the 2023 Netflix film *The Miracle Club*, three generations of friends travel to Lourdes, France, in search of miracles. The Grotto of Massabielle (or Grotto of the Apparitions), a famous pilgrimage site that attracts thousands of people every year, is the place where it is said that the Virgin Mary once appeared to a local woman and miraculously healed her.

In the film, the women travel to Lourdes for different reasons. A young mother wants to heal her son who doesn't speak; another wants to heal the painful lump in her breast. Those who seek healing dip themselves in a pool for a few moments, a kind of baptism to see if their lives change. Whether they do or don't receive some sort of miracle is left up to the viewer, but they all go home with new lessons on acceptance, friendship, and forgiveness.

I was particularly struck by a moment when the woman who is facing a possible diagnosis of breast cancer says that she knows her predicament is God punishing her for past sins. I've known this way of thinking. It felt very familiar to me, and I couldn't help but feel a pang of sadness for this character and so many real people who have lived with this image of God for generations.

How do we make sense of the world? Of pain? Of the things that happen to us, the things we feel we cannot control? We begin looking outside ourselves for answers, to a God in the sky or gods who have ruled for millennia. We try to find reasons for the things that happen so we can move forward. Each woman in the film was telling herself a certain story of what happened and what healing is (get in the cold baptismal waters and believe or doubt the whole thing). In the end, it seemed they each found something different, that maybe healing means showing up to your own life in a new way, changed.

It is difficult to attempt to write about the stories of religion and faith, and I will not pretend that I can easily summarize centuries of belief for us here. Like much of this book, I want to look at the story behind the story, at the *why* of what we believe and the narratives that move through us and around us.

I will, however, ground us in some of what I've understood from various aspects of religion, specifically the kind of Christianity that I grew up with in the Southern Baptist Church, which was largely rooted in patriarchy, sexism, homophobia, white supremacy, and colonization (you can read a lot more about my journey in my book *Native: Identity, Belonging, and Rediscovering God*). Understanding my spirituality as a Potawatomi woman who grew up in mostly white, Christian spaces is complex and has been a huge catalyst in leading me to embrace interfaith relationships and ask big questions about what we believe as human beings and, in relation, what we believe about the earth and the creatures around us.

Our religious upbringing begins at the micro level with our families—with beliefs, values, and ways of understanding the world and the sacred around us passed down to us by our kin.

While religion and many of our faith practices happen at the mezzo and macro levels (in large communities and even at the societal level), religion is also found and formed in the intimate dimensions. Think about the words of Jesus as he reminds us that faith can be as small as a mustard seed, meaning that, perhaps, seeds are more powerful than we give them credit for, just like the acorn that grows into a mighty oak.

> The idea of the male monotheistic God, and the relation of this God to the cosmos as its Creator, have reinforced symbolically the relations of domination of men over women, masters over slaves, and (male ruling-class) humans over animals and over the earth.
>
> —Rosemary Radford Ruether, *Gaia and God*

The above words from Rosemary Radford Ruether reflect so many of the stories of religion and faith, especially monotheistic ones with patriarchal societies, in which we've adapted to a Zeus-like god and favored him over relationship to the earth, to our neighbors, and to our kin.

In the Christian evangelical religion I was raised in, faith was all personal—personal sins, personal commitments, personal salvation, personal shame, personal, personal, personal. So, the people I didn't save? On me. The sins I committed on a daily basis? On me. My selfishness? All mine. This story was a seedling buried deep inside me, a story told to me over and over again, a story I began telling myself about what kind of relationship I should have with the God of the universe.

Religion is powerful because it is steeped in *story*. It's powerful because it is cultivated by cultures, in families. As Elise Loehnen writes, "Culture is contagious: we pass it on to each other like a virus. It permeates everything. No one wholly invents themselves. Culture is whispered into us, transmitted through almost every interaction."[1]

Religion is truly micro *and* macro and can bring tremendous change to families and communities around the world. We hold that power carefully, because culture is contagious, as our spiritual beliefs, practices, and stories are.

When I read that line about culture being whispered to us, I get chills, thinking of the insidious ways that extreme or toxic religious beliefs make their way into our lives as children. We hear the whispers, over and over: *Are you good enough? Are you pure enough? Did you do enough to be loved, forgiven, seen?* And, of course, these whispers come not just through religion but through school and work, where we are taught to achieve through *doing* instead of *being*. In adolescence, these stories begin to run very, very deep.

One of the most profound television shows I've watched in the last few years on the struggle with religious identity is *Vikings Valhalla*, which tells the story of the complex religious and social interactions—specifically between Christians and pagan cultural and religious identities—between 1002 and 1066, during the Viking Age. It's a fictional retelling, so of course there are holes and creative explanations of complex topics, but it gives space to imagine what these interactions may have been like and to remember the violence surrounding their stories.

It brought up so many questions for me, especially as an Indigenous woman, about the "paganism" of my Potawatomi ancestors *and* of my Celtic ancestors. Truly, stories like these *should* bring up questions for all of us as we ask what it might mean to come from peoples all around the world who have been deemed "pagan" and thus bad by broader religious narratives.

The story of religion has moved across the world, across time. Reza Aslan says in his book *God: A Human History*, "The entire history of human spirituality can be viewed as one long, interconnected, ever-evolving, and remarkably cohesive effort to make sense of the divine by giving it our emotions and our personalities . . . by making God *us*."[2]

This statement could terrify us, but I don't think it should. *Of course* we find the sacred through our own humanity. *Of course* we try to figure out the world through the lenses that make sense to us. The danger is when religion becomes the way we justify hate and abuse, the way we twist the name of a god to fit our want for control and power. Howard Thurman writes in *Jesus and the Disinherited*, "A religion that was born of a people acquainted with persecution and suffering has become the cornerstone of a civilization and of nations whose very position in modern life has too often been secured by a ruthless use of power applied to weak and defenseless peoples."[3]

In the time of the Doctrine of Discovery, European Christian men were given permission by their religious and political leaders to take any lands they wanted in the name of God. This meant that my ancestors, and other Indigenous peoples around the world, were immediately othered, considered less than, their spiritual beliefs and the origins of their stories somehow not enough.

"Pagan" comes from the Latin word *paganus*, meaning "villager, rustic, civilian," and *pagus*, which refers to a small unit of land in a rural district. Theodosius coined the term when he ruled the Roman Empire, differentiating between Christians and non-Christians, more specifically using the term against Celtic and Germanic peoples, and over the years this term has been used to "other" those who do not follow what the Christianity of the Roman Empire deems the right way to understand God or the world. This is a story, particularly of Christianity, that continues to create a reality of supremacy, and it's incredibly dangerous. I want a spirituality that is humble, is grounded, values childlikeness, can be felt in the heartbeat of Mother Earth, a spirituality that practices kinship, care, and belonging with everyone and everything.

I don't want to focus only on the ways religion and faith practices harm us (there are entire books on that, and you should be reading those too). I want us to remember that our faiths, our spiritual paths, our religious realities can offer stories of immense healing. Eckhart Tolle, in his book *A New Earth*, reminds us of the realities that come from the stories of religion we let become our lives: "All religions are equally false and equally true, depending on how you use them. You can use them in the service of the ego, or you can use them in the service of the Truth."[4]

So it goes with beliefs, with the stories we tell and carry, with the ways we interact with the world around us. When used for the truth, for love, stories of faith are like tiny sprouts carefully growing, stories that begin in our precious childhoods and grow to teach us to understand the rights of other beings.

In the summer of 2024, I spoke at the Chautauqua Institution in New York, on the land of the Erie and Haudenosaunee peoples. It was the 150th anniversary of the founding of Chautauqua, and I was honored to be there with the interfaith dialogue series to speak on how we can be caring resisters.

That week, I met and spoke in the series with the Venerable Tenzin Priyadarshi, a polymath monk who is the president and CEO of the Dalai Lama Center for Ethics and Transformative Values at the Massachusetts Institute of Technology. He gave his keynote address the afternoon before I did, and I was so comforted by and grateful for the way he spoke about the reality that we are all contemplatives. Asking what that means for our full humanity (not just our particular religion) is key to changing the world. He shared about the importance of the micro, the moments we hold within ourselves, the ways we value self-transformation.

Like Priyadarshi, I believe that so much of the work we need to do to change societies begins with us, around our tables, in the corners of coffee shops and our favorite reading nook at home, in our personal sanctuaries where we learn how to pray and why.

Priyadarshi shared about activists and saints who are deeply rooted in their interior life, and I remember feeling a sense of relief, like a page in my own story had been turned.

In that sacred moment, I had the freedom to remind myself that it's okay to focus on the micro. It matters to focus on the micro, because the mezzo and the macro—the community and the society—will always be there, loudly telling stories, loudly proclaiming what we are to believe.

Let's remember that an oak tree can drop up to three million acorns in their lifetime. That's like three million micro stories in a big, big world. Imagine the possibilities of how many stories are held in the world, how many seedlings we may tend to over the course of our own lives. This tender season of adolescence, of young life, is the time when we make decisions about who we hope to be in the world. Let us not take that work lightly.[5]

Only we can practice transformation; only we can decide how we show up in the world, what beliefs we hold. What we choose *will* shape the circles of influence around us and will ripple out. Those stories matter, and it's up to us, each of us, to choose stories of love and belonging over stories of hate—even and especially in our religious communities, our spirituality, and our faith practices.

When we understand the sacred as profound, enduring love, we can see the hurting world as in need of love and not missional evangelism, kinship and not judgment. We can use faith and spirituality to shape the world for the better, to tell a more loving story of the relationship between The Sacred and the people, however that shows up.

As we raise the kids in our homes, communities, and neighborhoods, we get to be honest about how religion harms and how it heals. We get to critique our stories and our ways of understanding, practicing kinship with one another as we ask who or what or why God, or The Sacred, is.

This, in turn, helps us practice love in the world, and that's beautiful.

At some point in our lives,
we declare that we are
going to find God, going to
explore the world and
demand an explanation
for all that has gone wrong
and all that we desperately
hope to change along the way.

How does one find God, exactly?
Where do we look—
because, at the end of the day,
what makes one place holy
and another place secular?
What makes one person saintly
and another one heathen?

Perhaps, at the end of the journey,
we find only mirrors—
mirrors on walls, in the
eyes of other humans, in the
presence of every living
creature, in the touch of
a tree's rough bark or
the swell of an ocean's wave.

Quite suddenly, we are
aware of our own,
beloved smallness.

And quite suddenly we realize
that we were never meant
to find God, whatever God is.
We were meant to acknowledge

that we were always, always
the mirror ourselves, hands
over our hearts, looking
into The Sacred and understanding
that The Sacred is looking right back.

7

RETURNING TO OUR BODY'S STORIES

I'm sitting at my desk, mid-morning, on a fairly balmy winter day. The sun is shining through the south-facing window of my office, and I hear hawks calling to one another just a short distance away. I imagine them swooping, dancing across the air from pine tree to pine tree, surveying the landscapes around and below them. I struggle to write words like this, so I close my eyes to focus better. There are so many distractions right now, even the sounds of roofers working on two houses on our street. Their rhythmic tapping is lulling until it isn't, and I struggle again to find center.

Words are incredibly difficult to access sometimes, even for us writers. When social media spaces began to occupy our brains and we wanted those dopamine hits more often than not, we made a trade—the slow and steady pull of a cleared mind and heart for an algorithm that is never satisfied, a transactional relationship with people we will likely never meet.

But it's not just the algorithm. It's me too, constantly trying to fill my mind with everything but the simple sound of the hawk's cry, with interviews of rock climbers and words from other poets, with documentaries about the world and what I might make for dinner tonight. It's beautiful stuff, the stuff of stories and relationship and what it means to be human, but it is noise nonetheless. I can hear the soft breathing of my two dogs, one of them patiently waiting for me to feed him lunch.

But I need to linger here, just a minute more, and decide for the first time in a long time not to look at my phone as soon as it buzzes but to stay quiet, eyes closed as I type these words, trying to simply find embodiment, senses engaged but not overwhelmed, spirit aware but not overloaded. These are the words I need today, the safety I long for, and no amount of clever marketing can make up for the sustainable, long-term habit of word-finding, of excavating what is deep within ourselves so we can see what might be waiting to rise to the surface of our bodies, to make their way from our center through our arms straight to the keys, words forming something around what our soul's intent might be in this moment.

I pause and wrap my arms around myself.

Email apnea is a thing I was told about once, a thing I googled because it sounded so ridiculous. But it is real, this reality of work-related apnea, and sometimes I notice it, when I stop taking steady, deep breaths as I work, when I put my body into stress unintended for it. The line between positive and negative stress is extremely thin in my case, the moment between energy and anxiety so quick I never catch it before it hits. So as I wrap my arms around myself, I lay my head back against my office chair, close my eyes, and take a few deep breaths. Being a writer is completely and utterly rhythmic, a dance between entering in, blazing like a fire, and letting the fire burn bright for a bit. Then, simmering, it moves us toward rest and recovery. It is exhausting and holy, and there is nothing like it in the world.

But this moment can't last forever. Cars drive by; a large truck bumps across that same road outside my window. The hawks have traveled to distant trees and skies, and, yes, the dogs need to eat. I enter back into the world of overloaded thoughts, trying to be a better sifter of those thoughts, trying to categorize what's most important and what can wait until tomorrow, until next week, until . . . forever.

I take a deep breath, asking it to honor this time for me and to help me return when I am without words again, when my mind and my world are too muddied to move clearly. The breath responds back with a resounding yes, and my body gives thanks for every circumstance that brought me here.

I wrote the short essay above on a day when I was desperately trying to write—and couldn't. It happens sometimes. What happens when the storyteller can't find the story, when things are foggy, when we are tired and feeling hopeless, burned out, or afraid?

We return to our body again, to our grounding. We remember that the words themselves matter and bring us back to life again and again and again.

In 2024 I visited New York City, just an Amtrak train ride away from Philly, a few times for speaking events. This was a big deal for me, because prior to that year I'd been to NYC only one time, and I was still pretty terrified. New York is beautiful in so many ways—the cultures, architecture, food, history—but for someone who struggles with anxiety and is sensitive in a number of ways, it can be sheer overwhelm.

I leave the speaking event and head straight back to the hotel room, turn the lights down low, watch TV or take a nap, drink glass upon glass of water to feel some semblance of care for myself, and try to prepare for the next time I have to step outside and calm my nervous system again.

When I return home from New York City, back to my people and my spaces, back to my dogs and my garden and my daily rituals, it takes about a week for my nervous system to find its way home again, to settle down and understand that things are as they should be. It's taken me years to accept my sensitive body and spirit, to speak a story of kindness to myself, and to acknowledge that even in my adolescent years I was this way, trying to make sense of a loud world as best I could.

The week after releasing my second children's book, *Summer's Magic*, I was really feeling this reality, and the words that kept coming to me were "my social battery is so low right now." These words came as an effort to understand myself better, to tend to the child in me, to listen to my nervous system when she says she is exhausted and trying to recalibrate takes some naming, and it also takes a refusal to shame.

In finding ourselves, we have to face expectations—the expectations others place on us, whether family or society, and, in turn, the expectations we place on ourselves. For years I wanted to travel, work, and find my daily rhythms like everyone else, until I realized how unsustainable that was. I shared once on Instagram about the realities of being someone with a sensitive body and a sensitive system, and so many others shared that they felt less alone in reading that.

When we seek to find ourselves and name things for one another, for ourselves, a level of fear shows up. *Why can't I just be an extrovert like them? Why can't I be confident like them? Why can't my body be strong like theirs?* We begin to tell a story that harms us, that frames us as the oddity, the thing outside the norm, the one who's just *too much*.

As we move forward in this book, I want to disrupt this story, to prune this seedling back a bit so that we can remember that how we show up in the world—with our delicacies and our strengths, our ways of being that disrupt the status quo—is sacred and worthy of celebration.

In my teen years, I was the only child still at home; my siblings were off to college, and I had a room and space to myself. I bought a huge board from a home department store, and my stepdad, Steve, attached it to the wall above my bed. Every few months, I'd redecorate my giant mood board to reflect where I was in life and where I wanted to be. You see, even then I was pruning. I was tending to my stories, to the seedlings of those stories, deciding what could stay and what might go. I was making space in my life for new narratives in ways I didn't fully understand then. Having this steady routine was magical and intimate, a rhythm only I practiced, a rhythm that changed my life. I had a safe place to be when my social battery ran low and I needed respite from outside expectations.

Ritual for Those Whose Social Battery Is Running Low

Find a safe, quiet space where you can dim the lights or sit with as much cozy darkness as you need. This ritual is simple and is meant to be as expansive as you need, to take as long as you need—again, we are letting go of expectations, aren't we? This ritual is focused on the 4-7-8 breaths: four counts breathing in, holding for seven counts, and releasing for eight counts. Close your eyes and relax your shoulders, your limbs.

As you breathe in, breathe in an expectation placed on you, by yourself or someone else or by society.

As you hold the breath for seven counts, imagine the expectation swirling around, getting broken up inside you, losing its attachment to your psyche, your soul, your being.

And as you release for eight counts, imagine that expectation leaving through your mouth like you're blowing out smoke, and it dissolves into the air, a complete release and letting go.

Repeat this with at least five expectations.

When you're done, let your entire body relax, take a few more deep breaths, and slowly open your eyes to the world with a renewed sense of tenderness toward yourself and others.

When we take the time to find ourselves, we begin telling a better story.

We cannot get an oak sapling without an acorn producing a taproot. This is important to remember as we think of the stories of adolescence. We grow in this stage of life because there is a strong root or set of roots digging deep and grounding us before we get to where we are going. How does the taproot hold on as the acorn becomes a sapling? How do we hold on to our origin stories as we continue to grow? How do the stories in our lives take root?

When I was an adolescent, I took a sex education class just like every other kid in my school. It was taught by a Christian organization, so it was mostly focused on abstinence and all the bad things that would happen to us if we had sex—lessons based in fear, fear, and more fear.

We girls were taught about having a period once a month and how to manage it, but there was no exploration of the vast, beautiful and sacred ways our bodies worked. If anything, we were taught to dread that time of the month, to be afraid of it and to be prepared for the struggle once it came. Along the way, lie upon lie brought cautionary tales of what could happen if we chose to give away our one precious gift, our virginity, and ruin the blossoming flower that is, essentially, all that we are.

We carry trauma in our bodies. We know this. And so often, that trauma happens in the close-knit spaces of our lives, in the tight communities or family systems we are a part of. How do we know what is safe out in the world if we don't know what safety means in our intimate spaces? How do we know to celebrate and trust ourselves when we aren't taught to honor the vastness of our own bodies and experiences?

Stories of fear can be liminal for us, or they can be lethal; they may lead us to look deeper into things we were once unsure how to acknowledge, or they may cause deep destruction and disguise the ways that fear controls the narratives we practice in our bodies, minds, and spirits. Fear dominated my life for about three decades, and it took beginning to listen to and trust my body to finally name that. I've written about fear and anxiety before, like the story I share in my book *Living Resistance* about my fear of water and the steps I took to overcome anxiety, if only for just a few minutes at a time.

Every time I go to our climbing gym or we climb outside at the New River Gorge, where we often go as a family, I assess my relationship to fear: *How am I feeling about this trip? How will I perform at the gym today? What kind of fear am I carrying in my body that I'm not even aware of? How is it going to show up, and when fear inevitably does show up, how do I work through it or with it instead of against it?* Even a short hike from our car in the parking lot to an outdoor climbing area can bring up a lot of deeply hidden emotions that remind me of fears that reach all the way back to my childhood. Usually, I need to stop and take a few deep breaths.

I grew up in a family full of traumatized people, and we did not know how to communicate that trauma or manage the fear around our circumstances, and we certainly did not know how to stop and breathe. So I learned how to hold on to a need for control, I learned how to please others over listening to my own needs, and I learned how to be very, very afraid.

I will say this to anyone reading these words and feeling their own fears rising: It's okay to be afraid! I don't want to be void of fear, because fear can teach us a lot about what we need, what we don't need, and where we are currently existing in this world.

What I want for myself, for my kids, for so many of us is the power to recognize fear, to work through and *with* it and to come out stronger and more resilient on the other side.

The other important thing to recognize about fear is that so much of it lives in our bodies, where our stories are often riddled with self-hate and societal pressures around the idea that if we are thinner, we will be happier, or, as Elise Loehnen writes, "If you get the thighs you want, you'll finally be happy, safe, accepted, over some invisible safety line of belonging."[1]

We are judged for living freely in our bodies, mocked if we don't fit the standard of what a body should be, depending on the gender norms placed on us. As much as I love being a rock climber, I see the horrific effects of body stigma in the gym, in young people who are in the competitive climbing scene and, like many athletes in various sports, put pressure for performance on their bodies, no matter the consequences.

Let's pause and remember our own taproot, the taproot that anchors and nourishes the stories we tell and the stories we're told in the communal spaces we are a part of. Let's ask questions of the stories told to our bodies and in our bodies, noticing fear and disrupting it, acknowledging the care necessary for our nervous systems to thrive. We need to pause and pay attention to the stories we tell about our own body, our own trauma, our own experiences, and hold space for others to share theirs as well.

8

A MAZE OF STORIES

Labyrinths are found on almost every continent on earth and have been featured throughout literature. They are powerful symbols and sacred sites. Labyrinths are communal, yes, to remind us of our connections to one another and to Mother Earth, but they also bring us into ourselves and into our own inner journey.

A labyrinth journey I went on in 2023 helped me address intergenerational trauma in my family and my Potawatomi ancestors who walked the Trail of Death. I share this story to remind us of the important work necessary for an oak tree's growth, from an animal finding an acorn and burying them in the dirt to the taproot that sprouts, allowing the sapling to grow.

The journey of growth, the journey of tending, is always a labyrinth, a sacred maze we move through.

In September 1838, over eight hundred Potawatomi people were forcefully displaced from Indiana and walked to Kansas in a two-month trek called the Trail of Death. Those people were my people, and I did not return to the land they'd been forced from until I became an adult.

At an event near South Bend, Indiana, in 2022, I shared about Indigenous resistance in America. So much of my work is about helping people reorient themselves back to the lands and the waters around us, back to Mother Earth, and it's also been part of my own personal journey of embodiment to face my fears of the world and to find myself again.

I grew up between rural Oklahoma and the deserts of New Mexico, moving back and forth between the two until I was about eight years old. Many of my early memories are wrapped up in some sort of imaginative play with Mother Earth—singing to trees, reenacting my favorite Disney scenes in open desert spaces, watching stars show up in the sky, pulling "stickers" out of my feet after playing for hours barefoot outside our trailer. We were poor, but somehow it didn't matter when the world held me so dearly.

As I got older, I lost some of that magic. I think many of us who grow up in America are told at some point that to become a good member of society, we must learn how to get a job, balance a checkbook, and forget about magic and play. It's one of the biggest mistakes we make, and often we return to the lands around us to find our way home again.

When I returned to Potawatomi land for this trip to South Bend, I was returning for so much more than that. The Indigenous story is about constantly searching to understand home, constantly finding ways to heal our connection to Mother Earth when colonization continues to take so much from us. This wasn't my first time near the Great Lakes, but it was my first time visiting in September, marking the month the Trail of Death began. A commemoration and a grief enveloped me as I settled my feet to the ground for a few days.

One afternoon, I took a walk on the campus of a seminary that had been built on a trading route between the Potawatomi and Miami tribes, the Bodewadmi-Myaamia Trail. In that space, my body felt timeless and strange, like I was floating and attempting to tether myself to the land for the sake of ancestors I'd never met, and grieving for the journeys they couldn't take in that very place.

While walking, I found a shaded area where a small labyrinth had been mown, an invitation to journey toward no real destination, a beckoning to go on a spiritual trek of sorts. I'd walked a long path around the campus earlier but hadn't noticed the labyrinth. I began the walk, listening to Gregory Alan Isakov's newest album in my headphones until I realized I needed the quiet to get my mind to settle down and let my body find its rhythm.

I walked the path, thinking about every ancestor, every Indigenous reality that forces us to find our way back home to our bodies and our lands again and again. These lands hold histories of colonization, everyday realities of grief that we cannot always see. We must peel back the layers of history. A labyrinth teaches us to do the same, to peel back the layers of ourselves to find what's underneath with the help of Segmekwe herself.

Eventually, I came upon a series of small switchbacks, and as I walked them, I thought about the switchbacks I'd recently hiked at the Red River Gorge while on a family climbing trip with my partner and our two sons.

The point of a switchback is to make a difficult trek easier, especially in a precarious or steep area. As I walked the tiny switchbacks of this Indiana labyrinth, I felt the reality sinking into my bones that every time I climb with my family or practice embodiment, I'm making the healing journey a little more manageable, a little more stable, a little more gentle.

Because the truth is that colonization can feel like the steepest, worst part of a climb, the most painful on every part of our bodies, our minds, our souls. The labyrinthine switchbacks, the gentle turns, the friends we make along the way—they are what help us get to our destination.

In September 1838, more than eight hundred Potawatomi people were told that their home was no longer theirs, that their ways of living were not acceptable to the status quo being built up in this country. Again and again, we hear this story, again and again, the trek becoming brutal and cold, and we ask if home will ever be home in the ways we need it to be.

Halfway through the labyrinth, I found a quiet spot to sit down and rest. I was shielded from the bright sun, that same sun that shone on my ancestors all those years ago, that shines on all of us, no matter who we are. Autumn was beginning to turn the trees to their brilliance, bringing death and hibernation in the coming months.

The truth is that returning to the land of my ancestors is scary. It's scary to acknowledge the continual power that colonization has over so many of us. It's why we fight for the lands, the waters, our creature kin. It's why we go on walks and climbing trips to find ourselves. And if we get the chance, we turn our fears into the powerful work that keeps us going, writing books, following our dreams, and upsetting the status quo.

I knew that climbing meant something to me when, one night in late summer 2022, I dreamt of climbing. I dreamt about it so much that I didn't sleep well that night, because even though I was climbing in the dream world of my mind, it felt like my body was too. As I dreamed, I faced fears I hadn't faced before.

When I began climbing earlier in 2022, I found that I had never faced many of my fears in a healthy way before. Practicing movement and embodiment pushed me to my limits, slowly but surely confirming something new about the way I was or wasn't loving myself.

Climbing was jumping into a world I'd always hoped to jump into, but I was still unsure if I'd stay. My partner, Travis, has loved climbing for years, and we all wondered as a family if it would become *our thing* or just *his thing*.

Until that night and those dreams, when I woke up exhausted the next morning and knew that this journey was becoming a part of me.

I was walking a labyrinth and didn't know the destination, every switchback challenging me but bringing me forward, step by step.

I bought a necklace from an outdoor store on a trip during our first year of climbing. The silver pendant strung on brown string contains an image of a woman standing on a mountain holding a walking stick. When I saw it, I saw myself. I saw this journey I'd started for my own well-being, realizing the ripple effects it had in my family and in the world around me. Maybe I also saw my ancestors, the Potawatomi women who marched from Indiana to Kansas to Oklahoma, who didn't give up on their dreams or their identities, who were practicing resistance and embodiment every step of the way for future generations.

I dream a lot, vivid, deep dreams, and I can tell when they are the ones that matter, the ones that are revealing something to me about myself, about my own hopes and fears. In the dream world, I'm a climber facing my fears. In the waking world, I am a woman facing my fears.

While resting beneath that maple tree by that Indiana labyrinth, I thought of a hike I'd taken a day earlier, thanking the flowers that had bloomed and were slowly turning brown, the pollinators catching every last drop of sustenance they could get before the cold arrived. Every moment we ground our bodies with the existence of the land and those who have tended to it for centuries, we are finding our way home, all of us.

I took deep breaths to calm my body, matching a gentle rhythm with the heartbeat of the land around me. When we want to become playful again, when we realize how much of the magic we've missed out on as adults, we go outside. We play in water, we ski slopes, we climb mountains, we hike and golf and play tennis. We are all, somehow, trying to find our way back to the possibility of a playful existence where we can feel free and at peace, connected and fulfilled, where we can dream and imagine the world anew.

What a tender space we are entering into here, where the story is no longer a small, easily manipulated acorn. The story is growing and becoming, busting out of their safe shell and being ushered into adulthood, going out into the world. Leaving behind adolescence is no small thing, and this is why cultures across time and throughout the world make space for this important season in life, honoring it and those passing through it.

Adolescence, heading toward adulthood, is a difficult space to be. We are trying to decide between individualism and connection; we are learning that grind culture is real and demanding, but we don't know how to stay away from it because we are being told a story that we have to push to be successful.

In adolescence, we're scared that we'll take the wrong path, or that we won't find love, or that the wrong job will leave us unhappy. We carry so much here, the stories swirling around us—like thousands of acorns scattered on the ground—making us dizzy with dread or anticipation, we aren't always sure.

"One of the best pieces of advice for young people is, Get to yourself quickly. If you know what you want to do, start doing it. Don't delay because you think this job or that degree would be good preparation for doing what you eventually want to do. Just start doing it."[1] David Brooks, in his famous book *The Second Mountain*, isn't making the case that young people forgo college and do something else; then again, he isn't *not* saying that either. His book, just like this one, is about the seasons of life we find ourselves in and the journey we take along the way, the pruning and trimming of the tree sapling, the way we pay attention to the story.

I think about the people whose stories I see on shows like *MasterChef*, who make statements of this nature: "I've lived my whole life with this other job, and it was never really my passion, so I'm quitting to finally do what I love." There's a valid argument here for choosing a job that we need versus a job we love. It's a tricky space to navigate in a society where we tell stories about what it takes to succeed.

The question is, What story do we choose, and how does that story live on in us? What stories do we carry of land, of grief and love, of hopes and dreams for what's to come? As we grow, who are the people helping us take care of our own stories, our own being? Just as squirrels and birds transport acorns, burying them in just the right spot, people help us move our stories from here to there, help us walk the maze of narratives that make up the world around us. Who are the people who take our hands, moving and mobilizing us toward shelter and the next season of life?

When we doubt the sacred stories of our bodies or our belovedness, what people and communities help tend to these stories, tucking us into safety and giving us space to become?

An ancestor sees us
before they even know us,
and sends forth something,
maybe a blessing or
maybe a curse, a reminder
that the journey didn't begin
with our birth and won't
end with our death.
Life is simply
a celestial revolving door
of beginnings and
endings, stories held in the
hearts that usher them through
our very lives, creating
the foundation for every
new generation that breathes
long after we are gone.

PART 3

SAPLING

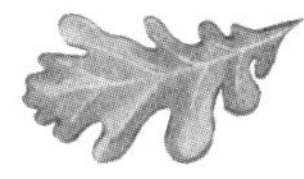

As long as we're too comfortable, too opinionated, too sure we have the whole truth, we're just rock and thorns. Anybody throwing us seed is just wasting time.

—Richard Rohr, *Everything Belongs*

Communities Tell the Story

As Story gets older, they begin to understand that
their thoughts and actions have consequences,
so they try to pay attention to who they surround
themselves with.
They know that change can be very powerful,
so they practice expansive beliefs,
trying not to limit themselves or others,
trying to withhold judgment.
They practice kinship and belonging.
They draw healthy boundaries around their heart
because they know that the world needs both
consideration and care, where healthy people
love one another well within their own abilities.
Story longs to be someone who loves well,
and every day, they are creating that space.

9

STORIES OF AGING AND HAPPINESS

Now we begin to see the oak tree grow, entering into what we'd consider adulthood. This is where we imagine certain stories outgrowing themselves, taking on new shapes and sometimes even new identities as they encounter what we often consider a midlife crisis.

This is the mezzo space in which stories are maturing through community. These are the stories of people coming to love their aging bodies or of those who realize they haven't been honest with themselves or their communities about who they want to be but now, finally, are breaking free of labels. At their core, these are stories of bravery and exploration, and we should celebrate this stage in life. Here we are like oak trees that have seen their fair share of weather and have housed animals and have brought shelter to the weary. In adulthood, surrounded by community, we are touched to the core by moments and experiences that change us.

Let's think about aging, specifically for women, because this is where I notice a lot of conversations happening lately. In their book *What Fresh Hell Is This?*, Heather Corinna writes on the topic of midlife: "How do all of us . . . usually know so much less about something so much more common . . . that will absolutely happen to everyone born with a uterus and ovaries in some way at some point . . . than we do about things less common?"[1]

Menopause is making its way into mainstream conversation (again), and I am grateful for that as someone who has struggled with hormone imbalances for years without having even hit perimenopause. In 2023, Oprah Winfrey and Drew Barrymore started up the conversation around menopause, and not long after, Barrymore became a brand ambassador for a supplement company. As you'd expect, there was both excitement and outrage—when we look into something as important as midlife for women, we also face that we live in a capitalistic system where there is money to be made by companies who can supply something we are looking for, a fit for our exhausted bodies. We are fed a story, and that story is that we need this supplement, this pill, this diet or food regimen to successfully get through the stage of life we are encountering. The wellness industry isn't just about wellness; it's also about money.

Sharon Blackie writes about "hagitude" in her book by the same name. We are "hags with attitude" when we hit the age when we shift and change, becoming another iteration of ourselves, living inspired by the feminine mystics and goddesses across cultures and literature who guide us.[2] My twelve-year-old noticed one evening at our climbing gym a few years ago that I have more gray hairs than I used to have on my head, and his first question was, "When are you going to start dyeing your hair?" "Never!" I obstinately answered, explaining how excited I am to let my hair go gray on its own. We talked about the pressure that women feel as they age to appear younger and how society punishes women who upset that status quo.

That small moment in the climbing gym revealed to me the stigmas around aging for women. We feel it all the time when a new commercial for antiaging cream comes out or we pass yet another plastic surgeon billboard on the way to the grocery store. Everywhere we go, we are reminded of our aging, yet, at the same time, rarely are we given helpful *and healthy* tools to navigate the seasons we find ourselves in or the hormones that play such a big role in our lives.

In 2021, I began having more open conversations with my kids about my hormonal life, about menstruation (which I called "mommy owies" for a long time), and about what it's like to be a mother and a woman. Around the end of that year, I began feeling really unwell and finally faced the fact that I had many symptoms of PCOS, polycystic ovary syndrome. I was finally diagnosed in early 2025, and have continued this multiyear journey of learning about balancing my hormones with healthier foods and movement as well as trying to manage everyday stressors.

Here's the truth: I wasn't even *telling* a story to my body; the story was just living there, and had been for years, silencing what my body needed. I believed the story that my body just doesn't work right and I can't fix it, that I should ignore the pain and hope it gets better one day.

I didn't even learn that my body has a monthly cycle of seasons until I was in my thirties. I didn't know that we have a relationship to our hormones that changes as we age. I didn't have any language or a handbook to help me figure out my own body. I'm still incredibly angry about the silence and misogyny that so many of us have experienced—in our school systems, in our health education classes, in our churches.

Like all stories, we move through cultural cycles, and right now we are in a cycle where conversations around menstruation, perimenopause, menopause, and conditions like PCOS are being shared widely, and I'm really grateful for that. Hormonal conditions like PCOS and the stages of perimenopause are still greatly under-researched and underdiagnosed, and we have a long way to go in honoring the stories that menstruating bodies tell. I had the courage to begin my own journey toward healing and discovering I had PCOS because a friend of mine shared about her own struggles on Facebook.

When we learn to listen to our bodies, we may not get answers right away, but we get a new story, one that has been calling out to us for a long time.

In fact, Indigenous women around the world are leading the way in decolonizing our ideas about menstruation. In an article titled "Decolonise Your Body! The Fascinating History of Māori and Periods," Leonie Hayden writes about the ways colonizers suppressed women's bodies and forced matrilineal cultures to give up practices that were essential to their cultures, including honoring the monthly cycle. She writes, "Secrecy is at the centre of all Western ideas around menstruation, just look at the advertising around it—from the baffling use of blue liquids to the active, glowing white women in white bikinis, this blatantly distorted image of periods implies only one thing—how you feel about periods and how you deal with them is wrong and weird."[3] Instead of giving in to these stories of how periods and menstruating bodies are portrayed by the media, women are harkening back to the ways of their ancestors, celebrating their bodies' cycles and doing so in community.

I think of Skywoman, who fell pregnant from above and suddenly found herself held steady on the wings of a flock of geese. The geese saw Skywoman in need and, in community, gathered to usher her safely down to Turtle's shell. *This* is the vision I hold on to, of care and connection and the simple, beautiful reality that we don't journey alone. Those who menstruate need communities to gather around them, and we need spaces to talk about our bodies without shame or fear.

The PERIOD movement, founded by Nadya Okamoto, seeks economic and social justice for young people and those who menstruate and promotes gender equality through conversations, stories, and awareness. It has partnered with actress Jessica Biel to write a children's book on menstruation, which reminds us that we have the power to shape the stories that come into our kids' lives.

In my own Potawatomi tribe, the Kwek Society, founded by Potawatomi citizen Eva Marie Carney, has set out to end "period poverty" in Indigenous communities across the country. Getting period products into public schools and healthy body-wisdom into the bodies and minds of young women is incredibly important for the world we want to build and the stories we want passed on to future generations.

As an adult, I am still doing a lot of healing around the stories I told my body based on the conservative Christian spaces I grew up in. The work takes a lot of time, a lot of kindness and care, a lot of sensitivity and honesty. Over the last few years, simply changing my eating habits and finding space for movement weren't enough—I had to actively engage the work of embodiment, to find power in my own body in a way I was never taught to before. I had to go deeply within myself to heal the connection to my inner child, embracing her with fresh vision. I had to ask what it means to constantly connect with Mother Earth in a decolonized way—a way that centers intuition and ancient wisdom. I had to find my own power *there*. I began rock climbing, facing my fears, showing up for myself through empowerment and care, and learning to manage stress as an act of resistance in a stress-fueled society. *This* is facing the stories we've carried and showing up to the power that is waiting for us.

Let's change the narrative and shift the story. Let's become fully aware of our bodies' seasons without being told (usually by male doctors or other health professionals) that we are imagining things or that we are too much. We are sacred, no matter what, in all the ways we change and transform. That's the story we choose to tell.

You've waited all
that time to finally
get a diagnosis,
only to find out
that the diagnosis
isn't the road map
you've been waiting
for—you are.

All this time, your
embodied soul,
your soul-filled body,
has been sending
precious messages,
holding out the
cosmic compass
that will guide you
toward your healing.

Now you have a name,
now you have a starting
point, a place where you
can get in the boat, where
you can set the compass
and begin the journey home.

But remember, it was
always you, always
you looking out to the
North Star, always asking
the waves to take you
exactly where you
need to go to get
to the destination
that was always
waiting in the

tender moonlight,
as she shushed and
shooed the waves back
and forth, as she tended
to your beloved body and
told you to keep going,
diagnosis and all, toward
the home of your belovedness.

Not too long ago, I watched the Netflix series *Live to 100: Secrets of the Blue Zones*. "Blue zones" is a term coined by journalist and *National Geographic* fellow Dan Buettner. He looked into places around the world where people have above-average longevity, asking why and how that might be. In the series, he identifies five unique blue zones around the world, each with various lifestyles that bring about longevity and better life values. Buettner argues that changing people's environment, rather than their minds, is what leads to longevity of life.[4]

For example, Buettner visits Nicoya, Costa Rica, which is not a wealthy area by global standards, yet the people there are living long, fulfilled lives. Don Ramiro, a 102-year-old centenarian, talks about his daily life habits, the things that make him and his family happy and connected. It's the *plan de vida*, reason for being alive, knowing your purpose in life and following it, that brings happiness and fulfillment.

The series urges me to ask what my *plan de vida* is, what matters, what I'm willing to spend my money and time on, and why. What stories do I tell about my own life and worth?

Right after watching that Netflix series, I read *Build the Life You Want* by Arthur C. Brooks and Oprah Winfrey. I admit I'm a little skeptical of books on happiness, often wondering whom they are *really* written for. Do we have to pay for our happiness?

Is it really a state of mind? Is happiness even real, or is it a story concocted by society?

What connects these two projects, and how do we look at the stories behind them? In the world of wellness and self-help, we love titles like *Secrets of the Blue Zones* and *Build the Life You Want*. These words cause us to pause and ask, "Am I really happy? Can I live longer? What will help me maintain a better life?" Isn't that what so many of us want? Being happy and well is one of those core stories that we are bound to as human beings. The two projects reveal our human longings.

Blue zones, according to Buettner, have four keys to health:

1. practice activity: move naturally
2. hold the right outlook: daily rituals, purpose, faith
3. eat wisely: incorporate a plant-based diet if you can
4. connect with others: build community[5]

Similarly, Brooks and Winfrey share four pillars of happiness:

1. family
2. friendship
3. work
4. faith[6]

Remember that the story has entered the adulthood phase of their cycle of life. In our midlife, in adulthood, the emerging stories are about our health, about getting a little bit older, about what our faith or spirituality means to us, about how we connect to others and what we might pass on to future generations, and about how our happiness is centered on family, friendship, work, and faith.

These projects bring to mind the idea of "third places." When we don't have family close by geographically or we aren't relationally close to them, or when we've transitioned out of a community or have left friendships or faith spaces, we begin the search for a space where we truly feel held and seen, a place for health, happiness, and connection.

The term "third places," coined by Ray Oldenburg in the 1990s, refers to spaces that aren't work, that aren't home, but that are *other places* where we feel welcomed, where we can be ourselves.[7] Think of the show *Cheers* or a local coffeeshop where regulars visit multiple times a week. I first read about third places in 2023 and realized I'd found one when I joined the climbing gym.

Third places perhaps began as gathering places for men who wanted to hang out with other men outside their homes, while their traditional wives stayed domiciled with the kids. Thankfully, things have changed. Third places can be diverse in a number of ways and bring people together who might not have otherwise found one another, providing a space for stories to overlap in community.

I hadn't had a third place in a while, because a few years ago we left institutional church spaces and have also moved every few years to different homes, neighborhoods, or cities. So stumbling upon my gym—becoming a climber and slowly building a community of love, welcome, care, and friendship—was a beautifully overwhelming experience. This third place at the gym was also where I saw women of all ages climbing, women talking openly about embodiment and empowerment, something I'd never experienced before. My climbing gym isn't just a gym; it's an art venue, a gallery for local talent, a place where my teenager plays Dungeons & Dragons on Wednesdays, where my youngest sold LEGO sets he'd built at home, an office, and a workout area—it's all of these things for people who need it.

I grew up being told that the church was the most important space—Wednesday night Bible study, Sunday school, youth group. For many people, church (or any religious space) truly is that third place. Yet for many of us who challenge religious institutions, we've entered our thirties or forties and left those spaces to find safety—and even happiness—somewhere else.

The oak tree reminds us what community is. There are over four hundred species of oak trees, and they are home and host to communities of animals, insects, and birds who depend on them. We, too, live in webs of connection and kinship, our stories woven into spaces that we hope to never forget. And when we face the midlife crisis of community, asking what it means to belong and to find happiness and wholeness, we begin to ask what stories we choose to tell about one another.

10

STORIES WE TELL ABOUT ONE ANOTHER

The stories we tell about one another can be incredibly powerful. Eventually, they can outrun us before we're able to stop them. To illustrate this point, think of one of the most insidious aspects of high school: the rumor mill.

Someone starts a rumor about another person, specifically to embarrass them or harm their reputation. Perhaps it's harmless enough, although the era of social media makes rumors far more accessible and disastrous for those targeted.

The rumor begins to spread, first to core groups of people, then to the school, then to the community. Families find out; folks at the local diner are heard talking about it over their breakfasts. Before anyone can stop it, the story has outrun the original teller, the creator—expanding and affecting more and more people as it grows.

This may be a dramatic example, but it's happened countless times. We watch television shows and movies or read books based on real moments just like this. Some people outlive the rumors told about them, and some don't.

It matters how we tell stories about one another.

This is where we begin to consider ideas of "othering" and "belonging." My book *Native: Identity, Belonging, and Rediscovering God* delves deep into the topic of belonging from an Indigenous perspective. What does it mean to truly belong in a world where we cannot always control the narratives told about us, to us? How are we responsible for the stories we tell?

Here's another example of the ways we talk about one another: Some kids are bad, while some kids are just having a bad day. Spot the difference? Certain people who carry out mass shootings are just evil, but people who struggle with mental illness can't help it. Spot the difference? When we dismiss the complexities of fellow humans, we are doing the dangerous work of labeling stories as lethal when, in fact, they may be more nuanced and in need of our love and care.

Like a rumor started by someone, stories told about those on the margins that demonize or infantilize them are often told by those with the loudest or most noticed voices and become lethal stories—the ones that live on the longest and end up changing the history of a place. I vaguely remember learning about the Capitol Crawl disability rights protest on March 12, 1990, when thousands of activists crawled up the steps of the US Capitol, putting on display the lethal and outrageous realities of inaccessibility in our country.

That day, thousands of stories of love came bursting forth, demanding to be heard and challenging the lethal stories that were bringing death and destruction to their communities. The Americans with Disabilities Act was passed that June. Today, disabled voters demand their stories be told at polling places that aren't welcoming and spaces that still aren't accessible. These lethal stories, the ones challenged by stories of belonging and love, go beyond physical accessibility—we have internalized ableism everywhere in our stories, and we need to recognize that.

Alice Wong, activist and creator of Disability Visibility, writes powerfully (and wittily) in her book *Year of the Tiger* about her struggle with internalized ableism: "Eugenics isn't a relic from World War Two; it's alive today, embedded in our culture, policies, and practices. It is imperative that experts and decision makers include and collaborate with communities disproportionately impacted by systemic medical racism, ageism, and ableism, among other biases."[1]

Eugenics, based on ideas of controlling populations by selecting those who are "worthy" of breeding, is incredibly dangerous and literally life-threatening. As Wong states, eugenics is embedded in policies and practices, and the way to recognize it and work to disrupt it is to work with those affected by it.

Our biases—like racism, ageism, and ableism—show up through the stories we perpetuate about one another. Can we catch those stories before it's too late? Is it possible to disrupt a story, to help a story change direction before more pain is caused? I believe so. I hope so. I hope the very pages of this book help you find a way to disrupt these kinds of lethal and oppressive stories. Our kinship connection to one another demands it.

Indian country looked to the 2024 Oscars with great hope. Lily Gladstone's nomination for best actress in *Killers of the Flower Moon* had so many of us hopeful that she'd be the first Indigenous woman to win, based on the trajectory of her award wins up to that point.

We were rightfully disappointed when she didn't win and the award instead went to Emma Stone for *Poor Things*. Those watching the announcement could tell that people in attendance were stunned that Gladstone didn't win, and for Indigenous viewers, the loss brought a reality of heartbreak, followed by anger.

I woke the next morning to the news, and I cried while standing at the kitchen counter packing the kids' lunch boxes. I felt exhausted and frustrated the rest of the day, even while remembering the immense amount of resilient fire that Indigenous peoples carry.

I took to social media before I turned to the pages of this book and shared a note with my Indigenous kin:

> *I don't know about you,*
> *but I felt heartbroken this morning.*
> *Then I felt the anger.*
> *Then I remembered our resilience.*
>
> *You can be sure that Lily is going to keep going.*
> *Her fire will keep burning, and her legacy will keep building.*
>
> *So keep being angry and bright and bold.*
> *Keep living resilience.*
> *And lean into all the powerful ways you move in the world.*
>
> *We need you.*
> *We need us.*
> *Don't forget that.*[2]

The reality of being Indigenous and aware of the settler gaze, or working in industries that are, of course, colonial to their core, is a difficult one. We have appreciation for and support the organizations and institutions we are a part of, but we also have to remain dedicated to keeping ourselves tethered to our cultures, our voices, our legacies.

What I've voiced in the publishing industry—about helping other women, especially Black, Indigenous, and other marginalized women—Lily has voiced in Hollywood. We get in the door, and we hold it wide open for those coming after us, making a way, challenging the status quo of colonialism. My friend Peggy Flanagan, Minnesota's fiftieth lieutenant governor and enrolled member of the White Earth Band of Ojibwe, says the same thing, and I constantly picture it—a line of us opening doors for the next woman to come through.

Lily's nomination (and her growing success in mainstream Hollywood) is a huge win for us in Indian Country, even if she didn't win the award. The powerful thing about working for our stories to be heard is that when they aren't, we let the fire burn brighter.

The morning after the Oscars, we woke up to a world still full of rage and hate, a world where the powerful hold so much against the powerless. Those in Gaza were still starving at the start of Ramadan, a sacred and holy season. Haiti was still reeling from gang violence. The United States was still facing a harrowing election season. The list goes on and on, because it always does.

A simple Oscar snub might not seem like much, but it was at the center of our Indigenous rage and exhaustion and, somehow, our immense hope too.

After I cried, after I got angry, I turned to the working pages of this book. I wrote and remembered that as Indigenous people, we have always been here. I think all the time about those Cowboys-versus-Indians storylines, how so much of America has been framed by this particular story, by the way countless films and now television shows portray Native folk as "merciless Indian savages," as taken straight from our Declaration of Independence.

Vandana Shiva wrote a beautiful foreword to the new edition of the book *Grandmothers' Wisdom*. She states, "Separation and superiority create structures of violence against nature, women, and every 'other' defined as lesser beings, with the objective of colonization. Inequality and injustice are rooted in the false assumption of separation and superiority."[3] This is where we see cycles that are traumatic and toxic—cycles of othering, of separation and superiority that lead to violence, that lead to structures of colonialism. This is why holding on to stories of hope within these spaces, within our communities, is essential in the work that is ahead of us today.

Let's shift perspective a little bit, to the flip side of "othering," to belonging and community. What do stories of belonging and community look like—those liminal stories, those loving stories grounded in kinship? What tools do we have today to help us practice storytelling in a better way?

Social media can be a horribly toxic place, but it is also highly responsible for educating me on disability rights and ableism, climate injustices, racism, discrimination against queer and non-binary folks, sexism, and much more. For so many conversations, I am grateful that I have been in the learning seat, listening to folks educate me (and many others) on the realities of being a disabled person in society, or being trans and fighting for human rights, or encountering racism in their small town.

On social media, we are told to speak up loudly, but I find so much of the work is also to be quiet and listen, to share others' work before we form our big, loud opinions. I want to be a student before I try to become a teacher; this is a place of contention in many of our activism spaces. We've created a culture of quick fixes and fast healing, and that is, quite honestly, the opposite of the enduring energy we need to hold with and for one another in a constantly hurting and changing world. When I think of that long, enduring work, I imagine us gathered up in the branches of a giant oak tree to tell stories of love and belonging. But to get there, we have to climb the giant oak. We have to climb, one foot and one hand at a time, acknowledging that the journey is worth it. When we gather in the branches of the sacred oak, when we tell better stories there, those stories become a part of us. And when we climb down and journey back to our lives, we take everything we learned with us. *This is sacred, sensitive storytelling.*

The complex reality, here on the ground, is that we need people to listen and learn, *and* we need people to speak up, to shift and change narratives, to make room for more love and kinship in our world and in our communities.

In 2024, I spoke at a small gathering in Nevada at a retreat and vacation spot called Zephyr Point on Lake Tahoe. My second morning there, I walked down by the water to an area called the Portal of Prayer, an alcove built near the shore, surrounded by a small wall of rocks. It's intimate and quiet and truly seems to be the perfect spot to pray.

Prayer can feel tricky for me, as I've written about in both *Native* and *Living Resistance*. Whether we want to admit it or not, prayer is connected to the way we view one another, to our ideas of belonging and how we think God or the Universe is in relationship with us. I don't exclude myself from this view of prayer, as I wrote earlier; I believe we often use religion and spirituality to shape what's happening in the world to fit our will.

Did our sports team win the game? God ordained it! Did I pass my test? It was God's will. Is my enemy suffering? God must be on my side.

I approached the Portal of Prayer with some quiet respect and humility. Who am I to ask The Sacred for anything? I whispered words of peace—please give us peace—while acknowledging that people's proclivity for hatred won't change just because I prayed it would. I was in Nevada serving as a keynote speaker for a conference on how to hope for and create justice and peace and kinship in the world. How was I supposed to pray for that? How was I supposed to live in to that?

The reality often is that I show up to prayer with nothing to say but every guttural feeling imaginable. I had tears in my eyes. I wanted to fall down at that portal by Lake Tahoe, wrap myself into a fetal position on the rocks, and wail.

Why does it hurt so much to be human? Why do we destroy each other? Why do we tell stories that create such suffering? Why do we practice violence? Why do we disagree on what violence and peace even are?

Maybe prayer is just about acknowledging that we often don't know what the hell we are doing, and that's okay. Maybe prayer is for linking our arms together and collectively admitting that we are complicated human beings, living on a sacred earth that we have harmed. Maybe we start there.

Brilliant and Tender Universe,
you've held us and our stories
since time began and before that.
Teach us now what it means to hold
those stories like we'd hold a tender seed,
like we'd shape a quiet sapling,
like we'd climb a giant oak to see
exactly what the birds get to see.
May we show up to our lives with
tethers of kinship, holding us close
from bough to root, holding us
when we forget how to hold
one another with that same
brilliant tenderness.
Iw. (Amen.)

11

STORIES OF MYTH AND OTHERING

Lately I've been asking myself, Are all myths stories, or are all stories myth? It's a difficult question. Depending on the cultures or peoples you're asking it of, you will get different answers. The first thing that comes to mind in my experiences is my Southern Baptist upbringing and the belief that every part of the Bible (both Hebrew Scripture and the New Testament) is fully truth, fully factual. In the public school in my small, mostly Christian town, we were taught to think about everything through the lens of truth or lies, with not much critical thinking or nuance involved around those realities.

As an adult, I've come to value so highly those liminal spaces where things don't quite make sense, where we ask a lot of questions and don't get a lot of answers, where we wonder what's real, what's not real, and what is real *enough* to matter to us.

This is the power of story, of myth, of cultural exchanges throughout history.

Joseph Campbell says it like this: "Mythology is not a lie, mythology is poetry, it is metaphorical. It has been well said that mythology is the penultimate truth—penultimate because the ultimate cannot be put into words. It is beyond words."[1] The ever-wise myth writer and elder Clarissa Pinkola Estés says it like this: "In mythos and fairy tales, deities and other great spirits test the hearts of humans by showing up in various forms that disguise their divinity. They show up in robes, rags, silver sashes, or with muddy feet. They show up with skin dark as old wood, or in scales made of rose petal, as a frail child, as a lime-yellow old woman, as a man who cannot speak, or as an animal who can. The great powers are testing to see if humans have yet learned to recognize the greatness of soul in all its varying forms."[2]

How do we examine a story to figure out what is "myth" and what is "truth," and are they as binary as we imagine they are? Here, again, the liminality of story is incredibly helpful and reminds us that stories don't always have to be *factual truth* to guide us on our journey.

We want to believe in so many stories and myths, those tales of monsters and legends that tell us a little more about who we are and how we got here. Surprisingly to some, belief in Bigfoot and other beasts is more common than we'd think because we've always needed mythology to show us who we are and what we believe. I stumbled upon John O'Connor's book *The Secret History of Bigfoot* one day in a Barnes & Noble right after it released, and I am so glad I did. This book is witty, full of personal and communal stories, and draws us into an important conversation on culture and stories. In O'Connor's words: "There may be no more sacred expression of American exceptionalism than faith in a monster we've adapted to fit our peculiar view of history, unfalsifiable by facts proffered by science or qualified experts, and suggesting a medieval belief in the raw and violent power of nature. Perhaps we all need Bigfoot in our lives, whether we realize it or not."[3]

An Atlas Obscura article notes that belief in the "Yeti" (from the Tibetan root *yeh-the*, which loosely translates to "small man-like animal") traces back to pre-Buddhist religions but rose as Western mountaineers began to climb the Himalayas: "When the race to conquer Everest heated up in the 1950s, so too did the number of alleged Yeti sightings. Western audiences were hooked, eager for news of this evolutionary hangover halfway between man and beast. Perhaps it was comforting to think that there were beings beyond comprehension surviving at the ends of the wilderness and that, crucially, there were still enough wild places left to hold them."[4]

There have been stories of creature or monster sightings all over the world, stories passing through Indigenous cultures across North America, or what we call Turtle Island. We have stories of monsters in the woods, like the Wendigo of Anishinaabe cultures—those stories are used to keep kids in line, to remind us that we are not alone, to warn us of how we should respect the world we live in. Should we be sensationalizing these creatures or leaving them alone by simply honoring the lessons they teach us?

In *Living Ghosts and Mischievous Monsters*, Dan Sasuweh Jones collects ghost stories from different tribal nations, sharing in the introduction that stories of ghosts and monsters are "always close to us because ghosts are part of our daily world."[5]

The supernatural world, the thin veil, the portal between here and there, or the world of "myth" and ghosts and monsters will always be a part of our human experience. Still, we come again to this difficult question of truth and myth and whether it's important to distinguish between the two. Sasquatch sightings have happened enough that the Bigfoot Field Researchers Organization was established to keep track of and categorize sightings. Whether the sightings are valid or simply a figment of imagination, they have, in essence, become a true, cultural, communal story. It is a story that has grown and continues to grow, like an oak sapling that becomes the tree that shelters us, growing roots that reach deeper and wider to form networks of belonging. This story is one that keeps people connected, providing an industry of films and memorabilia to small communities through the wallets of tourists who visit popular areas for sightings.

But myths and stories shift over time, as does our treatment of people, especially those on the margins. I imagined there was some sort of connection between the stories of Bigfoot and the witch hunts throughout Europe and later America, and I ultimately found evidence from Europe in the Middle Ages showing that the idea of the "wild man" emerged to terrify children and adults alike. As was the case in the hunting and killing of women accused of being witches, religion played a huge factor in the treatment of wild men. As O'Connor points out, "Things got so out of hand that hunting parties, not unlike witch hunts, were organized to ferret out culprits: in most cases, folks living at the social fringes—the insane, destitute, those who'd committed or had merely been accused of a crime, or old trouts or curmudgeons who'd taken to the woods."[6]

Monster myths are meant to keep us at a distance from the "monster," the person or thing that is nothing like us, foreign, inciting fear because they are so different. Most times, the "monsters" are just people who have, for one reason or another, subverted the status quo, offended the religious elite, made fools of those in power, or caused the comfortable some discomfort. Then, sometimes, the narrative flips and the monsters become those in power who rule and control with hate, injustice, and oppression. There's an important and enduring story there too.

We find this story throughout literature: The one thought of as the villain is actually a misunderstood hero, like Maleficent in the 2014 Disney retelling of the Snow White story. It's a powerful film about looking to childhood wounds and honoring a person for what they've gone through and who they hope to become. Maybe, at the end of the day, the monsters aren't who we think they are.

When the very people we should be protecting become our monsters, something has gone terribly wrong, and it says a lot about the dangerous status quo of our communities when that happens.

In high school, I studied the Salem witch trials for a history project, trying to understand a piece of history that was fascinating to learn about and reveals a lot about religion, sexism, patriarchy, and colonial social norms in an era of change. I wanted to understand the why and the how, but because I was missing pieces of my own history with colonization and hadn't yet found the language for it, I couldn't fully grasp what the stories were telling me.

When I think of the witch hunts, I think of the women who became a threat to the status quo. Their presence and power were used as the catalyst for the outcry against them, often resulting in horrible abuses and gruesome deaths.

Celeste Larsen reflects on this in her book *Heal the Witch Wound*, drawing the connection between women of the past and women of the present and what it means to stand against the status quo: "Of course, we cannot forget that patriarchy, imperialism, capitalism, and religious intolerance are still major forces in our modern-day society—just as they were during the Burning Times."[7]

I can feel the tension many Christian spaces hold when I'm invited to speak and I ask those in attendance to write love letters to Mother Earth or to acknowledge the kinship ties they have with the creatures around them, relationships they were taught weren't real. This lingering tension echoes the call of Indigenous wisdom, of wisdom from around the world, like Celtic Christianity, in which we see that the sacred is everywhere in and around Earth. When I point to houseplants as sacred or say that animals teach us about our humanity, people initially want to jump in and believe, but their colonized faith beliefs hold them back. I can see and feel the "othering" happening as I step onto the stage and name what it means to practice my own Indigenous spirituality, as I claim that it's taught me more about myself than the Christian upbringing I practiced as a child.

As I feel the ongoing power of colonialism today, I remember eras we've lived through when othering was used by specific groups to claim power. For example, healers, midwives, widows, and others who were "different" became the targets for Catholic and Protestant churches in Europe who were fighting for power and could use the witch hunts as a way to gain control through that power struggle. Later, as the witch trials came to the lands now called the United States, in places such as Massachusetts, there were fights between the old Puritan guard and the burgeoning democratic society, all on the backs and lands of the Indigenous peoples, who had already been there for centuries. Those deemed "other" were also blamed for things like the outbreak of the bubonic plague in the mid-sixteenth century as well as "social ills like overpopulation, inflation, and food scarcity, which were escalating in Europe."[8]

A story took hold and continues to this day in the way healers are perceived, in the ideas of what it means to be "pagan" or "Christian," in what it means to find yourself othered by society and religious and political institutions. The stories told then—stories of othering, stories grounded in dogma and belief, stories that produced power and control—ended in the execution of thousands.

We read stories like that of Tituba in Salem, Massachusetts, missing her Indigenous culture in Barbados and teaching the girls she nannied about voodoo and stories from home.

We recall the story of a Black woman who was forced from her lands and enslaved by a man who became a reverend, who was targeted and cast out for missing home and trying to hold on to whatever was left of it inside her.

We remember Sarah Good, a woman who was poor and hungry, considered "other," also targeted.

We think of Sarah Osborn, a chronically ill woman who dared to stand up for herself and became a target because of it.

The status quo is built on stories that circulate in communities, that make their way throughout the world—the lethal stories, the ones that destroy people and cultures, that humiliate and deny human rights.

Even in the reality of human rights abuses around the world, we look again to the mighty oak, a being who has sheltered many over the centuries. When the people of the world are power hungry, stealing from one another's experiences, stories, and lives to feed their own, the oak trees are still there, perhaps on the edges of society, beckoning the weary to come and rest in their shade.

In 2023, I was sitting at a small coffee shop in Texas. An hour before I was to speak at a justice conference, I read about the witch hunts, the "burning times," feeling them burn through me. My anger seethed as I put pen to paper, as I remembered with an ancestral clarity what it means to be a woman and what it has meant throughout the centuries to hold our stories with sacred care and wisdom, even as we are hunted down for it.

I light a candle for you,
every single one of you,
whose bright lights were
snuffed out by a society
that did not want your power,
did not understand your mind,
did not value your spirit,
did not tolerate your exhaustion.
I light a candle for you,
because to this day
we have not forgotten
what it meant for you to
leave this hurting earth
where your bodies were bruised
and your spirits were mistreated.

Sapling

When I light this candle,
I send love to you as you
travel across the cosmos,
as your spirit continues to
burn brightly, a light they
couldn't fully put out.
When I light this candle,
I hope you remember
that you are sacred fire,
and even though society
discarded you all those years ago,
the ripple effects of your heart
and legacy live on in future generations,
reminding us that we, too, are sacred,
that we, too, are lights not meant to be
burned out, lights meant to shine
brightly in spaces where
they still wait with their Bibles,
torches, and crosses to snuff us out.

12

STORIES OF SPORTS AND EXPLORATION

I find it difficult to trace the history of what we now call "sports," activities involving physical exertion and skill in which an individual or team competes against another individual or team for entertainment. A sport can be anything from a traditional hand game or lacrosse in Indigenous cultures, to a bullfight in Argentina, to rolling a disk of cheese down a hill, to the mortal peril portrayed in the film *Gladiator*.

Whatever form they take, sports bring communities together in incredibly powerful ways; there's no denying that. Our stories are told through sport, our communities are bolstered when we succeed, and we vow to fight harder the next time when we don't. Many sports were born from Indigenous cultures, and they carry our stories in them. Chelsey Luger and Thosh Collins explain how movement, the most fundamental part of sport, has always been essential to Indigenous cultures and ancestors: "Through day-to-day work and play, whether harvesting food or having fun at a social dance, they moved. And during life's great transitions—those monumental human challenges that we all still face today, like aging and evolving into new stages of life—they moved."[1]

Today, Native athletes participate in sports for the value it brings to their communities, for their ancestors and for future generations. They participate for connection, friendship, and movement, and to cultivate enduring values. American sports carry these sentiments too, but what do we do with sports that can be caustic, toxic, and dangerous, like American football, which causes countless injuries (and some deaths) and encourages the use of offensive Native mascots? We hold, once again, the power of liminal stories in all their complexity, knowing that a sport like football can provide outlets for kids in impoverished communities while also injuring the players involved.

The Netflix documentary *Home Game* examines sports from around the world and the ways these sports have changed their communities and cultures through movement, stories, and risk. In the series, a fighter from Florence, Italy, shares, "Sure, money is important, but having a story is more important."[2] To many professional athletes, being part of the world of sports is about having something to pass on to future generations and, yes, in some cases, honoring ancestors.

But the way toxic or lethal stories can be passed through our sports communities is dangerous as well. Naomi Osaka, a Japanese professional tennis player who was ranked number one in singles by the Women's Tennis Association and was the first Asian player to hold the top ranking in singles, became vocal in 2021 about her mental health challenges (specifically depression and anxiety) within the sport: "In my case, I felt under a great amount of pressure to disclose my symptoms—frankly because the press and the tournament did not believe me. I do not wish that on anyone and hope that we can enact measures to protect athletes, especially the fragile ones."[3]

I was incredibly proud of her when I saw in the news that she stepped away from the sport for the sake of her mental health, because I've had to do the same in my own spaces. There is always this feeling that we are not enough or that our struggles are "all in our heads" and we can simply overcome them with the right attitude. This is the kind of colonial, white supremacist thinking that permeates everything in society, including sports.

Another important story in sports is that of Olympic bronze medalist rugby player Ilona Maher, who was criticized for not being "feminine" enough. As an elite athlete who struggled with disordered eating for much of her life, Maher shared about the effects of destructive body image messages and why it's important to advocate for *all bodies* to be accepted and celebrated at *all levels*.

I can only imagine what stories these women have been told—that they aren't enough as they are, that their bodies or minds or ways of being in the world aren't enough, or that even though they perform well in the sports arena, they aren't "performing" well in other ways. The narratives of judgment and the pressures that follow them are tragic and dehumanizing, and it's important to pay attention to the way these stories show up.

I didn't grow up with sports or appreciating healthy movement as a form of medicine, and it's taken me some time to understand how the stories of sports change communities. But today, as a mother and rock climber, I see how sports can play a part in my own family's life and overall wellness and what that might mean for the stories we tell.

Whether it takes place inside at a gym or outside at a crag, climbing is a sport. It is also a spiritual practice for some and a form of community for many. The climbing community has had its own journey, from conversations on body image issues for young competitors to British mountaineers who used Tibetan athletes to get to the summits so they could "dominate" the mountains.

Sport climbing in the United States has its roots in a vagabond group of (mostly white men and a few women) misfits who didn't want to follow the status quo of suburban America, including Royal Robbins and founder of the outdoor brand Patagonia, Yvon Chouinard. They settled in Camp 4, a basecamp at Yosemite, making their home in the shadow of El Capitan. This era of climbing is romanticized in many ways but has a deep story: People who didn't seem to fit into society found a home among the mountains and boulders outside and created a whole new movement from it.

When I think of climbing, I don't just think of those people in Yosemite in the '60s and '70s. I also think of the way climbing has changed and the incredible communities that are showing up to shape the landscape of the sport, like Brown Girls Climb, adaptive climbing groups, queer communities of climbers, Natives in the Outdoors, Latino Outdoors, and so many more. They are showing us what it means to tell a better story.

I think about how being a woman in the 1500s was risky, just like it's still risky today—we are constantly assessing what is safe for us to do and who we should be, constantly wondering what's at risk as we empower ourselves in societies around the world that don't value us. We must acknowledge that "the body and nature are both metaphors for the feminine: We must allow it to emerge, to reinstate it in a place of respect if not reverence."[4]

There's an interesting history here. Much of mountaineering and climbing has used the language of "domination" or "conquering," which I think reeks of colonization and supremacy. Instead, what if we viewed our exploration of the outdoors as an extension of our sacred relationship with Mother Earth?

The PBS Masterpiece series *Hillary* tells of a team of European (and two New Zealander) mountaineers who summited Mount Everest. In one clip, Sir Edmund Hillary is speaking to a British captain about the mountains, describing them as a woman, which, in my mind, produced a direct link to the story of power, the story of "conquering the feminine mountain," just like women have been "conquered" for centuries. This view of the mountains was so embedded in their psyche that they may not have even noticed it. That particular story became the status quo, a looping story that wasn't questioned and continues on loop today.

In contrast to this idea of conquering and dominance, the local Tibetan name for Everest is *Chomolungma,* meaning "Goddess Mother of the World," while the Nepali call her "Goddess of the Sky," which gives an immediate sense of reverence and respect. This is parallel to many Indigenous cultures around the world that honor Mother Earth and all the beings around us, like the Pennacook-Abenaki, who honor Mount Washington, or *Agiocochook,* meaning "home of the storm spirit." Mountains are sacred beings, and our interactions with them matter. British author Brigid Delaney asks, "Why do we still feel the urge to 'conquer' mountains? Why, in ever increasing numbers, are we scaling Everest, or continuing to climb sacred places such as Australia's Uluru in spite of the objections of traditional owners? Why are we venturing to the Galapagos Islands or taking a cruise ship to Antarctica to marvel at the incredible wildlife, in the knowledge that our visits there are assisting in destroying their fragile ecosystems?"[5]

Norbu Tenzing, the son of history's most famous Sherpa, Tenzing Norgay, says his father would be upset to see the circus that is modern Everest. In an interview with *The Guardian,* he shares the following:

> [My father] would be quite horrified with the way things have turned out. Since the time he was climbing there's been a complete change, a shift in the way people climb Everest and what motivates them. . . . The sense of people going on an adventure, working together, doing something nobody's done before, with a sense of comradeship and working together—that spirit doesn't exist now. It's just a total service industry, where you're fulfilling the egos of western climbers and people from south Asia who want to test the limits of how close they can get to death, at great expense of the Sherpas.[6]

Questions are important to ask—and stories must be examined again and again—because as much as we long to be adventurers and explorers in the world, those explorations have consequences. Becoming a climber as an Indigenous woman in connection to the lands around me has been important and complex, revealing to me a community of people who care about the lands around them, and others who don't always think about how their climbing affects others. As climbers, we have to ask, What does it mean to be in communion with the world around us, to engage in embodiment with the rocks and waters, to honor the peoples who have tended these lands for centuries?

Climber Mariana Mendoza advocates for decolonization within climbing, creating beautiful, collective conversations about what it means to climb as community and to engage with each other and the world through belonging. In an interview with the Center for Story-Based Strategy, she shares what she's passionate about: "The rock climbing/'outdoor' communities are mostly oblivious about their role in practicing and sponsoring settler colonialism, heteropatriarchy, and ableism. Most people in those communities don't realize they are dismissing reparations and social/economic justice. As a rock climber, I am responsible to create opportunities to challenge and change problematic narratives and open imaginations."[7]

As Mendoza and others advocate for this particular sport and community to tell and live better stories, we are finding that we get to live into the power of this moment, to expand our communities, to find the wisdom of the oak tree, which reminds us again and again that we are connected to one another in order to thrive.

As film director and climber Mikey Shaefer once wrote in a piece for *Climbing* magazine, "Climbing has always been more than just a sport. It's provided a way of life and a makeshift family to misfits who share a calling."[8] Expressions like this give me hope for the future and remind me of the power of stories and that we can be part of shifting them, shaping them, and living into them, including how climbing helps us live healthier lives.

Through climbing the last few years, I've been healing trauma to my nervous system, learning to manage anxiety and stress, and embracing what it means to get into my body and out of my head.

I am not the only climber who talks about the ways movement and climbing help with anxiety and other mental health experiences. Daniel Pohl, a climber who makes topography art for a place called Avalonia in Germany, shares about his mental health journey and how much solace and joy he has found in creating Avalonia and celebrating his relationship to the land and the rocks there. In one scene from the YouTube film *Stone Locals*, Pohl looks straight into the camera with a huge, sincere smile on his face and says, "We are children when we go bouldering."[9]

Pohl carved and thoughtfully curated space for climbers after leaving various mental health institutions on realizing that the systems created for people like him were consistently failing him, telling him a story about himself based in fear and self-hate. In climbing, he found his own childlikeness again. Among the rocks, he told his own story.

Even though climbing is becoming much more mainstream (even finding a home in the Olympics), it's often a sport for those who feel "other" in many social spaces, and it is still very much about connections to lands and the stories that live on those lands—stories of collaborating, care for Mother Earth, our changing climate, and climbing organizations and groups working alongside Indigenous peoples to protect sacred lands. Beyond climbing, we have a chance in outdoor sports of all kinds to honor a connection to earth and community.

Let us remember that the lands around us tell foundational stories, and if we choose to listen in community, we get to take part in shaping what stories end up forming our societies. We know that trees find their way in community—when one tree suffers, it pierces the ecosystem, the gentle and intricate web of belonging and care. We, too, find our way together, and show up and pray for love along the way.

Sapling

There are mountains all over
this land whose stories
are crying out from the
base of the rockface.

Continually now,
their voices are covered up
by our sense of adventure,
by our desire to conquer.

Whose stories remain?

What words, images, characters, lessons
are buried there in the cracks,
still holding on, breathing,
still speaking?

Look up from your lowly post
and maybe you'll feel it—
time holding the stories until
they emerge again.

And if you get close enough,
place your palm against the stone
and let the stories enter you,
breathe through you, become you.

Become a stone yourself,
a story-bearer, a witness
to every sacred word
written there in magic and choss.

PART 4

MATURE TREE

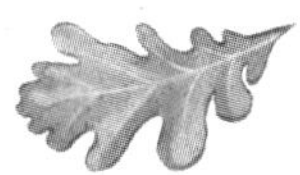

The only way you can change the world is with stories. And the bigger your legend becomes, the easier it is to share the story.

—Cristina Mittermeier,
Win or Die (documentary)

Societies Are Changed by Stories

Story relies on their relationship with Mother Earth,
moving about the world in ways that honor that
relationship, and encourages others to do the same.
As Story gets older and becomes an elder themselves,
they pass on the stories they learned when they
were young, in the forests, around the dinner tables,
in the quiet corners, beside the blazing fires.
Story helps the younger ones find their way,
and Story paves a path for future generations to grow
tall and strong like a mighty oak, always dreaming
of ways to plant new seeds of belonging.

13

STORIES ARE LABELS

As oak trees age, they often become hollowed out on the inside, making room for many different creatures to shelter in their cavities. I think of this as I imagine a story aging. Stories become so huge that they shape societies and leave us asking ourselves who is sheltering inside those stories—who are the shells giving safety to, and why?

Here we are at a very sacred time in life, elderhood. In this time, there is societal-level growth, which brings up questions about how exactly societies are formed.

It's important to remember that oak trees take years and years to grow—they peak at around 80 to 120 years old. Stories, like trees, take years and years to mature, to grow, to form and shape societies as we know them today. Think about the rings of an oak tree, what they tell us about age and health. So, too, a story has a sort of inner circle of rings. We can look back at old newspapers or trace oral stories through history to see how the shape of certain stories changed depending on who told them or how they were used.

Every now and then, as I'm looking through the many books on our shelves, I come across a few from the world poetry class that my partner, Travis, and I took in undergrad, the class where we fell in love. It was among a fabulously eclectic group of peers that we found ourselves, that our relationship blossomed, that we were reminded of our love of words and stories. Under the guidance of one of our favorite professors of all time (and still one of my favorite humans), Joy Dworkin, we studied not just poetry but the embodied lives of people like Rilke, Akhmatova, Szymborska, Neruda, and Baudelaire, among others. Poetry, like so many other forms of art, isn't just about the art itself. When we read a poem, we wonder about the how and the why behind the words.

I was so moved by Anna Akhmatova's "Three Things Enchanted Him," written in 1911, that I put it to music, a song that Travis and I still remember to this day. The poetry of Charles Baudelaire, who wrote during the industrialization of Paris, was criticized by many for being borderline "crude" about the realities of his day. Rainer Maria Rilke is a poet admired by many around the world, especially for his well-known "Letters to a Young Poet," in which he touches on themes of love, loneliness, being human, and the power of poetry. He writes in one letter, "Perhaps all the dragons in our lives are princesses who are only waiting to see us act, just once, with beauty and courage. Perhaps everything that frightens us is, in its deepest essence, something helpless that wants our love."[1] In those very words, a story is challenged. What if the parts of ourselves that we don't want to acknowledge, that we see as evil, shameful, unmanageable, are the parts that need our greatest love, the parts that want to be held, healed, and cherished? Polish poet Wisława Szymborska wrote of peace and war, themes that carry throughout history, that reverberate in our stories *and because of them*.

In my book *Native*, I write about the prophetic witness of poetry: "Poetry is life to us and to those around us. Throughout time, our poets are often our prophets, the ones who dance and sing and write, expressing things we did not know were stirring inside us for years. Our poets, our storytellers, are the bridge between the languages of the earth and our spoken languages, between the stories of the earth and our stories."[2]

Art is more than just *art*. Words are more than just *words*. And stories are more than just tales we tell. They are all alive, moving and breathing and prophesying among us. What do we make of that?

As a poet, I'm not keen on titling my poems. The same was true with my songs when I was a songwriter. Sometimes I even wrestle with titling my books. How do I title something, put a label on it, when I want the reader or listener to feel it deeply? Will the title, the label, take away from the story? Will it warp its embodiment, sending the reader or listener in a direction I'm not sure I want them to take?

Our lives are often labeled, split into sections to be understood. I sometimes look back on different life seasons in order to figure out where I was at each moment, and each of those moments in my life can be traced to the power of a story.

So what happens if the old labels aren't working anymore? What if I want to redefine things on my own terms and hope that, in doing so, I help others shed their labels and come fully into who they are and who they hope to be? What if, in the way of being a mystic, I want us to simply learn to listen to our own lives on a new wavelength?

Author Najwa Zebian writes in her book *The Only Constant* about the process our bodies go through when we want to change—in other words, when the old labels aren't working anymore and we want to be free of them.[3] But change is terrifying and can affect us on every level—in our bodies, our spirits, our minds. The challenge is to find ways to exist through the change.

When it comes to labels, we are finding ways to exist within the contexts we have created, on the macro level and in society at large. I think of history as a loop or even as the infinity symbol, a number eight turned on its side, with us somewhere in the middle, and future generations on the other end, all of us constantly moving back and forth around those lines and spaces, around and over one another. We are connected by the stories we tell. It's true, we cannot change what has already happened, but we *do* have a role to play in what happens for future generations, what unfolds for them.

Mellon Foundation president Elizabeth Alexander writes about belonging and resistance on a regular basis. As I write about in my book *Living Resistance*, resistance is also about labels. Alexander headed up the foundation starting in 2020, leading a $250 million Monument Project to take action across the country, with the goal of helping us tell better stories about the America we know. In cities where grants from the foundation are awarded, new monuments will rise up in place of old and offensive ones. These new monuments tell stories that aren't often told in the American landscape, stories that reflect the accurate and rich cultural diversity of who we are. This project reveals the truth about stories and how the societal labels we've placed on lands and peoples can come through something as simple as a statue. We know that the *kinds* of statues we erect can change the narrative of a place. Across Turtle Island, we have so many incredible stories to choose from that reflect the beauty of who we are and the lands we live on—let's let *those* stories live on.

In Mount Lemmon, near Tucson, Arizona, I went climbing in 2023 with a friend while on a trip to speak with Indigenous students at the University of Arizona. As we drove back to town, we passed an area called the Gordon Hirabayashi Campground, which I came to learn was this area's second name, based on the stories of what happened there. The area was once the Catalina Federal Honor Camp, where conscientious objectors to war and Japanese Americans were imprisoned, human rights advocate Gordon Hirabayashi being one of them, because he challenged the existence and injustice of Japanese internment camps by going straight to the FBI and turning himself in.[4]

Climbing walls in the area are still named after prison themes, which speaks to an issue within climbing culture and the necessity to revisit names of rock walls that perpetuate histories of violence. In Ten Sleep, Wyoming, a series of climbing walls were renamed in 2021 after attention was brought to their problematic and offensive names, like "40 Acres and a Mule" and "Slavery Wall." Whatever the intention or idea behind the name of a climb, it's important to pay attention to what labels do, how they work in society, and how they affect us. Climbing walls with racially offensive, violent, or sexist names should be changed for the sake of a healthier, more welcoming climbing community.

In some places, like Ten Sleep, the names were changed, but in other areas, there's still a lot of work to do. Just like we can take down or rename a monument, we can rename spaces whose names tell a story of pain, racism, and hate with a story that propels us toward love, inclusion, and care.

Iranian climber Nasim Eshqi uses the sport as a platform to advocate for women's rights, not just in Iran but all over the world. She shares about opening new climbing routes in different countries and using names that promote human and women's rights. In France, she named one route "Rise Up for Human Rights," and a second is called "Woman Life Freedom," a slogan of the revolution in Iran. She encourages the climbing community to name routes after activists and women who are changing the world. She says, "Everywhere in the world walls are very masculine, the lens is very masculine."[5]

Whether we call them lenses or labels or stories, they take on their own power, and we have to recognize that. They become the new trends around us, shaping the direction we're headed toward. Pulitzer Prize–winning journalist Jose Antonio Vargas writes about the labels put on immigrants in his book *Dear America*: "Migration is the most natural thing people do. . . . The difference, however, is that when white people move, then and now, it's seen as courageous and necessary, celebrated in history books. Yet when people of color move, legally or illegally, the migration itself is subjected to [the] question of legality. Is it a crime? Will they assimilate? When will they stop?"[6]

How we label history, people groups, their actions, and their lives lingers in the stories we tell, and as we've seen again and again, those stories are buried deep in the lands around us, the cultures around us, and even the foods we eat and the ways we explore our relationships to one another.

As my kids were starting fifth and seventh grade in 2024, we went out for an evening hike to clear our minds and get some energy out of our bodies. As we hiked, we played word games, explored old railroad tracks, meandered through the woods among elder trees, and, at moments, quietly thought about the coming season.

Elder trees are some of our greatest teachers. Sometimes when I'm in the presence of a tree that I know is aged, I pause. I sit in awe. I breathe in the air that they give a little more slowly, with a little more tenderness. Oak trees bear witness, they hold space, they mark moments in time with powerful awareness, and it is a gift to us human beings—the fact that their wisdom still reaches us.

What if we honored our elders this way, listening to their wisdom, which teaches us to pause and let go—of the labels, of the old things that no longer work for us, of toxic stories—in order to usher in movements of love? Our elders can help us prepare for the coming season, for the life waiting for us.

I wrote the poem below for my kids that night in the woods, as we were letting go of the summer that was slowly drifting into our past and asking what was coming and how we might change with the world around us.

Don't let go so quickly.
You can ease your way
into the waters of change,
one arm stroke at a time,
each breath a steadying rhythm.

Open your palms slowly.
Let transition trickle in,
eyes closed and spirit ready
for some new horizon
to sweep you into its sunrise.

Ready yourself for tomorrow.
The season will come as it should,
the world bringing you into
sacred, tender orbit, all things
ready to cycle forward.

14

STORIES OF LAND AND FOOD

I travel all over Turtle Island as a public speaker and workshop/retreat leader. I've been to small-town Idaho, college campuses in California and Boston, my ancestral home of the Great Lakes, the deserts of New Mexico and Arizona, Upstate New York, the dry landscape of Texas, the mountains of Lake Tahoe, and all throughout the Midwest. Everywhere I travel as an Indigenous person, I feel a precious and resounding tension, a clash, a melding, a dance—between stories, between cultures—and I wonder if we can ever get back to the way it might have been before.

The reality is that I see lands and waters tainted by empire while the Indigenous peoples who cared for (and continue to care for) them are forgotten or pushed out of both physical reality and history. Some gone; some still fighting.

Once, at an online event, right before it was about to start, the person in charge asked if I'd be giving the land acknowledgment because I'm Indigenous. When I said no, I hadn't prepared a land acknowledgment because I was not from the land where they were gathering, they quickly googled one and offered the vague, empty statement with no real action behind it. I was reminded that often even acts of remembering Indigenous people can quickly become a box to be checked instead of a way to truly respect and honor the people who have been on these lands for millennia.

How can we be partners? How can non-Native people come alongside Native folks to bring change and community to areas across Turtle Island and beyond? We have to acknowledge where we've come from, who we are, and where we hope to go from here. We have to enter into the power of story.

While in the Lake Tahoe region of Nevada for an event in early 2024, I met an elder of the Washoe tribe who shared about reclaiming waters and natural areas by using names in their traditional language. *Da'aw* is the word for "lake." He said with a slight grin, "When they [the settlers] named these waters 'Lake Tahoe,' they named it 'Lake Lake.'" We snickered like a couple of middle schoolers sharing an inside joke.

This is the way it is with the battle of stories, labels, erasure, years of history, moments of hope, recognition, reclaiming, language. Maybe it's a long cycle and we are just coming back around again, finding our way home to ourselves and each other.

I visited Da'aw one morning and wept at the pier. Every time I spoke, the waters seemed to respond, lapping at the edge of the dock with a sense of urgency.

"You're going to make it," I whispered.

The waves lapped louder against the dock.

"I'm sorry for how you've been treated," I said.

Lapping, lapping, reminding me of their presence.

"Thank you for loving us," I choked out through tears.

Roaring waters responded, because they know how to love us, and they do.

For a moment, the modern-day storyteller took over, and I wondered how I could share this on social media or in this book, how I could tell the stories, get people to understand. This is always our dilemma as storytellers—we are both experiencing the world *and* crafting words to describe it at the same time, because it's how we process and understand the shape of a story. It's how we make sense of the magic, the sorrow, the human experience. But Creator and Da'aw brought me back to the moment again, reminding me that not everything is meant to be a snapshot. I wept more, wondering how we got here, how so many stories have been lost, how, in the name of commerce, we've damaged ecosystems and sacred passageways without a second thought.

I think of Coldplay's Chris Martin, who, in an interview with Zane Lowe, Apple Music's global creative director and radio show host, shared how important it is for him to submerse himself in a body of cold water when he travels for shows. He says, "When you get in the water, it reminds you to be humble because you're just tiny again."[1]

For Martin, there is an ebb and flow to grounding fame, to being on tour in front of millions of people and also finding space to be in water and barefoot on the earth as much as possible. There is a beautiful story here about belonging and hope, and I feel it in the themes of love and hope in Coldplay's music. Their art is born from their relationship to the world around them.

There is so much work to do, but that doesn't mean I've run out of hope. Dr. Jennifer Grenz, in her book *Medicine Wheel for the Planet*, writes about a moment when an elder took her out to visit some plant relatives. She thought she was going to study, to use science and knowledge in the way she'd been trained, but the elder had other plans. Instead, they sat there, listening. They paid attention and had a sacred conversation that led them to so much more than what they'd imagined.[2]

That is what I experience every time I visit the waters and forests, mountains and valleys of a new place—moments that make me stop, let go of the words, sit, and listen in awe. Like a little kid who wiggles around too much, I try to steady my mind, my body, my heart. I try to soak up what's being spoken, to embody stories that have been forgotten.

The lands and waters around us don't hold just Indigenous stories, though. They also hold the stories of forced migrations, of families separated at borders, of immigrants searching for home, of people imprisoned and human rights trampled. They hold memories of weddings and celebrations, of babies being born and prophets changing the world right here, right at the shoreline, in the deep dirt being tilled on a farm that is being reclaimed and its stories decolonized.

Land is connected to people, to culture, to society, and, yes, to food. One evening, I was opening a fortune cookie with my family after we had eaten takeout from a nearby Chinese restaurant, and I paused for a moment, wondering where the idea of the fortune cookie really came from. What story was behind this cookie that we want every time we visit a Chinese food restaurant, which are such a staple in the culinary world of America? Are these cookies Chinese in origin? Or do they have another story connected to them? It didn't take much of a deep dive to find out.

Fortune cookies, as we know them today, are based on a Japanese wafer—a miso-and-sesame-flavored savory cracker—called *tsujiura senbei*, which originated in Kyoto in the 1800s. Jennifer 8. Lee, author of *The Fortune Cookie Chronicles*, says that the cookie is believed to have reached the United States when Japanese immigrants arrived in Hawaii and California at the turn of the twentieth century, "after the Chinese Exclusion Act's expulsion of Chinese workers left a demand for cheap labor. Japanese bakers set up shop in places such as Los Angeles and San Francisco, making miso and sesame-flavored 'fortune cookie-ish' crackers, among other treats."[3]

Eventually transformed from the savory cracker to the vanilla and butter-based treat we have today, this cookie is now easily customizable and sold by Wonton Food Incorporated, the largest manufacturer of fortune cookies in the United States. The company was founded by Ching Sun Wong, who emigrated from Guangdong, China, to the United States in the 1960s and started the business in New York City's Chinatown.

As with so many things, there is a story within a story within a story, like Russian Matryoshka or babushka nesting dolls, like an onion, like a labyrinth we walk. Which layer of the story are we encountering, and what lies beneath? In ten, twenty, thirty, sixty years, what story will be brought to the surface? What story will be most alive, most told, most believed?

This is how we get societies as well—groups of people brought together to form cultures and norms, value systems and beliefs. It is a marvel; it is also the root of so much pain and suffering in the world.

I've learned so many things since beginning to research for and write this book, and, as often seems to happen when we begin to lean into something, the theme started showing up everywhere. I learned, for example, that wine corks are made from the cork oak, found throughout the Mediterranean, another example of how essential the oak tree is to our world, to our societies. This is not just about the wine cork but about the stories that exist around it. How have those oak trees been taken care of, whose stories have been told in their shade, and whose have been ignored, covered up, pushed out of land and place?

The story of food and land is the story of colonization, the story of care and compassion, the story of displacement and finding home again. It's the story of the peasant farmer and the wealthy family, of the poor waiting outside the palace gates for scraps of food, but also of the communities who gather around tables to celebrate the seasons or milestones in each other's lives.

I read chef Dan Barber's *The Third Plate* in 2024, and while I was reading it mostly for my own enjoyment, I came to realize that it was helping me process the stories of land and food for this book, at least from Barber's perspective as a famous chef and advocate for sustainable farm-to-table practices. This book is full of gorgeous storytelling. One story centers on a *dehesa* in Spain, where Barber meets with Eduardo Sousa, known for his famous *foie gras*, or goose liver. When Barber meets Eduardo, he finds him to be in a beautifully tender relationship with the geese, not controlling with force when or how or where they eat but giving them everything they need to thrive, unlike many of the animal processing practices around the world.

A key to this landscape is, of course, the oak tree and the sweet acorn meal produced in the symbiosis of the grasses and the acorns themselves, providing a hearty and fatty meal not only for the geese but also for the famous Iberian pigs that live there as well. Extremadura in Spain, where the *dehesa* is located, is a land where many Spanish conquistadors grew up, a land that produces wool as well as the other foods I just mentioned. In the mid-1500s, the Spanish created a set of laws to protect the oaks on the land, with large fines for anyone who so much as tried to cut off a small branch.

Learning the stories of land and food is like following breadcrumbs to see where they lead. What happens when we tell one particular story? What happens when we change the narrative and go in a different direction? Even *one* story of *one* particular place can take on many different perspectives. So the next time you're at the dinner table or out at a restaurant with friends, pause to consider where the food came from, how it got to your plate, and what it means to your own story and to our collective stories that the items nourishing you literally traveled around the world to do so.

Michael Twitty, a Black, Jewish, James Beard Award–winning chef, writes in *Koshersoul* that "being Jewish and Black is not an anomaly or a rare thing."[4]

When we talk about food and explore our stories, we are exploring the ways that everything overlaps. The stories that unfold on the *dehesa* are important to pay attention to, just like the stories that unfold on a reservation somewhere as traditional Indigenous foods are being made, just like the stories that Twitty creates through the food he cooks. "Jewish food and Black food crisscross each other throughout history," he writes. "Both are cuisines where homeland and exile interplay. Ideas and emotions and ingredients—satire, irony, longing, resistance—and you have to eat the food to extract that meaning."[5]

When I make wild rice and berries, a traditional Anishinaabe meal, I am taken to a new place, connected to my ancestors in a way that can happen only through food. When cookbook author Reem Kassis writes about the foods of her Palestinian ancestors and family, like *za'atar* and watermelon, in her beautiful children's book *We Are Palestinian*, she is bringing the stories of her people to the world, acknowledging who she is, tethering herself to stories of hope.[6]

It is so interesting that stories are born in the dirt, in the land, in us, just like acorns take root in the dirt, in the land. And here we come all the way back around again, because as societies, as a global people, we have to look around and see where we should be returning to—to the land, to the dirt, asking what stories should continue to be cultivated.

The sign at Bedford Valley Road
said that to save the USA,
vote Republican, a story
we tell in hopes of making
a place more like ourselves.

The question is, of course,
Who are we?
What are we now, and

who have we been,
and who exactly were we
in the very beginning?

Because stories are like
growing trees, we must
keep watch before
they outgrow us forever,
a being that cannot be contained.
And we, young as we are,
won't quite notice our growing
until we're too far gone.

On another road in another state,
there is a sign on one farm that reads
"Hell Is Real"
and on another up the road that says
"Have a Nice Day,"
and I know which story I hope will grow
to maturity and which will be forgotten
in a land longing to finally know itself.

15

STORIES TOLD IN PUBLIC

We find ourselves, here, perhaps, at the crux of the story, the crux in the life of a story, in the life of a nation, of a people, of a planet. When stories have gotten big enough, like the stories of land and food, the stories of people and societies, we begin to ask how we got here. What stories are challenging each other to a duel, and who will win? What stories are reaching out to one another for community? What narrative will be the most important, the one that shapes everything from here on out?

The crux of a climb, the crux of a story, the crux of a birthing event is when everything shifts, when we feel immense pain and struggle because we are about to come out on the other side of all this pain and struggle, to find something there, hopefully something beautiful. I can remember those climbs, coming to the crux and wondering if I'd make it to the other side, if I'd finish the climb at all. I can remember while giving birth to my kids that moment when things got really, terribly painful, when I could feel it all, the suffering before the release.

Stories told in public become that sharp pain when narratives jab into one another and we see the struggle between hurting and healing all laid out before us. These are the moments when societies shift, when we know we are on the cusp of something. We felt it in the 2024 election season, when there was an assassination attempt on Donald Trump at a campaign rally in Pennsylvania and, later, when Biden stepped down and Harris stepped up. We felt it when Trump won the election in 2024 and began dismantling fundamental institutions in our young nation as soon as he began his presidency in 2025. We felt it when we asked how we keep telling stories of hope when things feel hopeless. We felt it with the rise of authoritarianism around the world, the battles between peoples and beliefs, citizens flooding streets to demand human rights and ends to war and genocide. The crux is when we show up to demand a better way forward and we fight all the way through the pain—together.

The interesting thing about a crux is that we don't know how long it will last. Time becomes warped there and even disappears from our psyche. The transition period in a birth might only be an hour, but time stretches to many hours as we hold on. The crux of a climb might be a few short moves, but we trudge through them. The crux of a moment in history might take years to get through, and we might not see the other side in our lifetime; yet we hold on and we hold steady. So here we are. Hold on. Let's see what happens next.

On Super Bowl Sunday 2024, I spent the early afternoon trying to enjoy my Sunday, but the reality kept creeping up that in just a few hours, a majority of Americans would be watching a game between the Chiefs and the 49ers, both teams that celebrate the Gold Rush (which took the lands and lives of many Indigenous peoples) and depictions of violence toward Native communities.

People often want to know what *really* bothers us about Native mascots and caricatures, and even though we've talked about it, written about it and protested about it, and there's been research done on how such images affect Indigenous young people, I'd like to explain the problem a little differently.

A few months prior to the Super Bowl, I was strangely surprised by a few conversations in which I heard people talking about playing "Cowboys and Indians," as if it were just a normal part of childhood culture in present-day America. The Cowboys-and-Indians myth lives on in the psyche of so much of America, whether we realize it or not.

The idea of the "Native savage" would be terrible for someone to express out loud, but the mascots and caricatures we see of Indigenous people (especially men) prove that we haven't gone far from this trope and that this toxic myth is still powerfully present and informs the way Indigenous peoples are targeted and treated by society.

Until we deal truthfully with the reality that even old movies create cultures that define us, we will have no reason to get rid of things like Native mascots at schools in tiny towns that no one knows about. It will forever seem like it's not a big deal. But remember, stories grow and shift and change, and kids today are still playing Cowboys and Indians, and Western films are still being made that portray Indigenous people as savages, and Native Americans are still fighting to be seen as something other than how these stories shape us as the enemy.

In all of this, we understand that art holds immense power, because at the core of art is storytelling. We've told stories through drama for centuries, on the stage and on the screen. We *need* those stories to make sense of who we are, and that's exactly what I've done throughout my life with the characters in television shows and movies, whether it was the family in *Family Matters*, the Olsen twins in their movies and as the character of Michelle on *Full House*, or the football team that faced down racism in *Remember the Titans*. I needed these characters to make sense of my own complicated life.

The screen portrays so much of our humanity back to us, in both beautiful and horrific realities, and we are inundated with screens everywhere we turn. Hop in an Uber and you'll probably see a screen attached to the seat right in front of you, in addition to the one that is already in your hand or pocket and the other one that is likely in your carry-on bag for the flight you're about to take. Our society is shaped by the screen, by the stories told on screens, playing in loops throughout our lives.

This poem that I wrote in 2024 reflects who I was then and who I still am today, and the power that stories hold through a television screen.

> There's a tenderly running joke
> in the family to get Mom
> a box of Kleenex nearly
> every time we watch a
> television show that
> tells a powerful story.
>
> It doesn't matter, does it,
> that it's a cancer-surviving farmer
> on MasterChef,
> or a single mom
> on an obstacle course,
> or two people reuniting
> after years of horrible separation?
>
> A story is a story is a story.
>
> So I hug the tissue to my eyes
> and remember the Cree elder
> who once taught me that tears
> are sacred, a thing to be held,
> honored, and treasured.
>
> I wipe my cheeks and
> hold the tissue close

to remember, and I
blow my nose and promise
never to stop crying out
to a good story that also
cries out to me.

With the invention of newspapers, then radios, then eventually televisions, humans have been the recipients of certain stories coming from certain angles, often confirming their already-formed biases. I think of the episode of *I Love Lucy* in which the Ricardos and Mertzes have given up trying to watch television, so they turn on the radio and begin staring at it, waiting for the story to begin. Lucy breaks everyone's concentration by pointing out that they don't have to *stare at* a radio because there's nothing to see, and they all start laughing at themselves, at the absurdity of being as transfixed by a radio as they are by the new and exciting television screen.

We have endless stories, opinions, and reports flashing across our eyes every day, affecting the way we think, feel, and act. Money is poured into ads that change our minds; corporations use their resources to get a message across however they can in order to profit off our emotions.

According to a 2023 Pew study, 32 percent of American adults got their news from television news sources; additionally, 56 percent said they got their news from smartphones, computers, or tablets.[1] As evidenced by newspapers shutting down or going completely digital, the era of getting news from radio and print sources is disappearing as online articles and social media—information on screens—continue to make their way to the forefront. This is often where we get our ideas on politics and news from around the world.

Even as the world erupts, we are quick to hop on to X (formerly Twitter), Facebook, Instagram, and TikTok, where we may be flooded with posts from a few actual news sources yet also overwhelmed with everyday people's opinions about what's happening.

It's important to differentiate the stories here, because a reporter researching a story is not the same thing as a civilian tweeting their thoughts on a topic, and we know that even reporters can tell biased stories. Social media has become a space that "broadcasts our voices, our mistakes, and our disagreements for all to see. . . . It can change stories, challenge the way things are, and, sometimes, sadly, it can tear things down."[2] How do we stop to examine a story, and what role does the media play in our changing world?

On a five-hour flight from the East Coast to the West Coast in 2022, I sat next to a woman who watched Fox News on her screen for the entire flight. She journaled to Fox, slept to Fox, read while Fox played, and I'd guess that she has it streaming in the background at home as well. As much as I tried to stick to my programming and ignore hers, I noticed the same ads playing over and over, the same messages, the same stories—all becoming fully engrained in the person watching. It's not just Fox News watchers who are inundated with certain messages. Depending on our political or social leaning, we all get what we're interested in through television and social media, thanks to algorithms creating a social bubble through resounding stories that lead us to believe even more deeply what we already believe.

Just as our cultural stories, passed from generation to generation, become a part of who we are, so do the messages we hear over and over again in the news become a part of our subconscious and even our spirituality, affecting our choices, whether we realize it or not. Once beliefs are ingrained, it's hard to step back and challenge them, and it can become a terrifying endeavor to decide whether to speak up once we've changed our minds.

In a 2023 piece in *The Washington Post* that examined this phenomenon of changing news outlets, the author stated, "News is consistent in that as long as humans and all their complexities exist, it will never stop happening. The ways we follow it, however, are changing quickly, and that can impact everything from how stories are covered to the way people feel about unfolding events."[3]

We have responsibilities as people who take in stories. But what is the responsibility of news outlets to ask themselves about the stories they are sharing and how those stories impact communities, nations, and the world?

The really complicated, confusing thing is that multiple stories are woven through any given society on any given day, and those stories get exposed by our prophets, poets, truth tellers, journalists, artists, and activists, while at the same time, governments and corporations around the world pay for ads, fake accounts, and comments that are meant to scare people into changing their beliefs and opinions. When governments, elected officials, or other powers in society are resisted or exposed by reporters and journalists, it sometimes results in death.

In May 2022, Al Jazeera journalist and American citizen Shireen Abu Akleh was killed in the West Bank by the Israeli army while reporting on a raid in the Jenin refugee camp. Also in 2022, Indigenous expert Bruno Pereira and British reporter Dom Phillips were killed as they were trying to expose the ongoing extractive industry in the Amazon.

How do we pay attention to stories told in public? I tend to be the type of person who listens before sharing an opinion, living as a sensitive activist. Author Dorcas Cheng-Tozun wrote a book called *Social Justice for the Sensitive Soul*, which helped me understand how I respond to news around the world: "Finding your place in the social justice sphere is not about conforming to someone else's version of who you need to be. It's not about contorting yourself to fit a particular role or activity that seems especially noble or effective. Finding your call begins with finding yourself."[4]

Here are some ideas on how to navigate the constant stream of stories being told on social media and in the news:

1. Listen, read, research.
2. Pause, reflect, ask questions.

3. Take in what others say without responding.
4. Spend time away from social media; process and discern.
5. If you need to share in a thoughtful and productive way, do so.
6. Ask how this news affects your life/community and how you can use your gifts to help.

Remember, we're in a space to examine how stories shape societies, and that's exactly the power that media holds. Often entire narratives are reduced to short segments or taken out of context. Following the steps outlined above (and adding a few of your own as you need) will help us determine what to listen to and believe in a world that is incredibly fast-paced and loud, where everyone is saying what they believe as the ultimate truth. It's essential that I, as someone who lives in a sensitive body and deals with overwhelm on a regular basis, follow these steps for myself, to sift through what's happening and to share the things I learn with others. And when we make mistakes, share misinformation, or live in reactionary ways instead of being fully present to how we show up in the world, we take a step back and learn from those moments.

In elderhood, we are still learning about ourselves. We can become older and wiser and still do the beautiful, tender work of unlearning. Just as the elder oaks continue to grow deeper roots and thicker bark, so the stories told in society continue to grow. We can still ask questions of the stories we tell in public and pay attention to the power they hold. We can still investigate a story when we come across one, asking how they are aging and becoming. And, yes, we can still change.

16

STORIES OF BELIEF AND LETTING GO

Just like many aspects of our identities, beliefs begin early in us. Whether they're religious beliefs, social beliefs, cultural beliefs, or beliefs about who we are as humans, beliefs are stories we tell, and they can be incredibly powerful—and incredibly dangerous.

John O'Connor explains the journey with beliefs like this: "The single most pervasive cognitive deficit we all suffer from is confirmation bias. Say you've told yourself a certain story. . . . Chances are you'll find evidence for it everywhere. Even the most counterfactual, contrary evidence won't dissuade you from your belief."[1]

Sticking to our beliefs can be both beautiful and terrifying. It can be beautiful and powerful to believe in something with all our hearts. But we all know people who won't budge on certain beliefs, who have been telling the stories of those beliefs their entire lives, or who have had entire lifetimes that primed them to believe certain things. When we look inward, we realize we have beliefs we refuse to let go of, even if we should, because we are afraid.

We desperately need beliefs in our lives, don't we? Whether we believe in UFOs, Bigfoot, a higher power, DNA testing, democracy, love, or one of many contemporary conspiracy theories, beliefs ground us to ourselves and to community. They give us meaning in life, a reason to do the work we are doing or to be part of the communities we choose to be part of.

The long-running television series *Survivor,* for all its serious issues (racism, ableism, fat phobia, and cultural appropriation), is a fascinating study in how people approach social issues and roles in light of their beliefs. Many of the social-based reality television shows out there today display this same concept.

Who is willing to uphold their beliefs and be loyal to their group, and who is willing to lie and manipulate in order to achieve the outcome they think they deserve or want? Who *actually* stays loyal to their core group, even in the face of elimination or at the risk of losing the one goal they've worked toward? Who honors their beliefs, their morals, even as they hold on to their goal to be the winner, and what biases and understandings undermine these efforts along the way?

The reality is that often our beliefs are directly tied to trust in certain people, for certain reasons. Up until college, when I finally became a voter, I was primed to believe that I should vote Republican because that's just what we did in my family and in many of the Midwest communities I grew up in. I didn't know another way, another option of belief, until I stepped further out of my community and decided for myself what my own beliefs could be. It's similar with religious and social beliefs that we may hold on to until suddenly we are changed by an experience, a friendship, a shift in life that takes us in another direction, to new people, places, and ideas. Moving to larger cities personally stretched me, slowly but steadily, into new ways of approaching the world, because my experiences became diverse, varied. New people in my life helped me ask questions I hadn't asked before or was too afraid to ask.

The deep trust we have in the adults in our lives—in authority figures like parents, teachers, pastors, law enforcement, doctors, and others—keeps us tethered to beliefs and often probably terrified to go against those beliefs for fear of what might happen socially, in our families and in our communities, if we do. Is it worth it to change our beliefs, to be part of a different story, to risk losing the people and ideas that matter to us? For some it is, and for others it isn't, and that's the tricky thing about being human.

An article in *Greater Good Magazine* of the Greater Good Science Center at Berkeley explains why it's so hard to get people to change their minds and beliefs. It comes down to a few core things: It takes work to change, it's scary to change, and there are consequences when we do.[2]

Our role as storytellers in the world is to ask what it takes to change, what belief should be about, and what we learn from ourselves and those around us as we transform throughout our lives. Some of the most powerful stories we come across are the ones that show that transformation is possible. We get to ask if it's possible in our everyday lives as well.

Let's consider three areas of life where beliefs are incredibly strong: politics/empire, religion, and our relationship to the earth. We are in the life season of a story in which empires have enough power to change whole societies, to make huge impacts on the entire world. Empire is a historical, repetitive choice, and it is about power and control. Entities, institutions, and persons in authority control nations, states, societies, and economies. My friend, the wise Jacqui Lewis, a Christian leader and interfaith advocate, reminded me one day of the Jesus who knew he was embedded in an empire and chose to exist within that empire anyway, chose to resist anyway, chose to tell a different story anyway. We get the chance to do the same.

The empires that have been built over the centuries that use police violence, oppression, unjust laws, and unfair power dynamics rooted in patriarchy, white supremacy, colonialism, and greed have made a lasting presence, and, yes, these empires include the United States. The terrifying question—Will the powerful always win?—rings in my ears every single day as injustice after injustice is displayed in the world. In the face of empire, how do we change our beliefs, knowing that it takes work, knowing that it's scary, and knowing there will be consequences?

We must remember that there is sacred strength in people gathering to tell a different story, to *live a different story*. It is powerful to wake up and practice kinship and belonging; it is powerful to challenge our own assumptions and beliefs, to ask big questions of our religions, our political stances, our identities. *That* is how we continue to exist inside of empires in holy, steady, beautifully subversive ways that lead to healing and love.

In his incredibly powerful and tender book *Surviving Storms*, Mark Nepo shares about the meaning of the word *radical*, which is "inherent, forming the root." In the plant world, *radical* means "return to the root," which for us means that "to be radical is not veering sharply from the norm but pursuing and returning to the intrinsic nature of things."[3]

I found so much hope in his words, because, in this light, being radical is similar to the way I describe the idea of resistance in my book *Living Resistance*: the way we use our everyday lives to exert energy against the dangerous status quo of our time. Resistance is not only what we are against but also what we choose on the other side of something or someone. In the time of empire, in the time of fear and hatred, how are we *radically resisting*? How are we using our everyday energy to return to the root, to ground ourselves, to get curious and show up to our questions, to challenge beliefs, and to celebrate change as it comes?

What about religion? How do our religious beliefs cement themselves in us, and how do they change throughout our lives, if at all? Religion is most definitely a seed planted in us but also one of the best examples of a story that can be traced from the micro to the macro, from the smallest, most intimate beliefs to something that actually controls the landscape of entire nations.

In the United States, there has been a rising fear among evangelicals about the "nones," characterized based on a Pew research study:

- Most nones believe in God or another higher power. But very few go to religious services regularly.
- Most say religion does some harm, but many also think it does some good. They are not uniformly *anti*-religious.
- Most nones reject the idea that science can explain everything. But they express more positive views of science than religiously affiliated Americans do.[4]

The study reveals the historical trend of the United States religious landscape related to other countries: "These projections indicate the U.S. might be following the path taken over the last 50 years by many countries in Western Europe that had overwhelming Christian majorities in the middle of the 20th century and no longer do."[5]

This is a serious topic, and I know that many Christians find it scary to imagine the faith fading away, people leaving the institutional church or no longer claiming Christianity. But we are also in a time of immense change, of challenging the status quo, of asking if we can be better than we've been and if we can let Christian supremacy be a lethal story we choose to stop telling, a narrative we choose to stop forcing on others. To many spiritual leaders, we are living in a time of deep spiritual awakening, a powerful moment to see how the narratives around us are shifting.

I've learned something significant as an author, public speaker, retreat leader, storyteller, and interfaith advocate over the last several years: People *do* change and long for the courage to be nuanced and expansive. And when those people do change, they go looking for others who are also interested in change. Some of these people are the "nones," the seekers who have been hoping to find spaces that welcome an expansive spirituality.

I've met people from all walks of life who have shared with me how much my work has shaped them, or how the work of my peers has helped them create lasting change within their families and communities. One reason I wanted to write children's books is because I know that change happens in families and communities through the children, through something as simple as a book—like an acorn, a seed—telling a powerful story and connecting us all to ourselves and one another.

I've been reading *The Seeker's Guide* by Elizabeth Lesser of the Omega Institute. Lesser takes the reader on a journey of seeking to understand the human spirit and the ways we examine the world around us, the relationships we hold, and the beliefs that continue to shift and change as we get older. Whether we are someone who identifies as "religious" or "spiritual," there is room for an expansiveness that we get to offer ourselves and one another. I think that's one of the greatest gifts we can give as we shift and transform in our lives.

Let's take a moment to remember that oak trees are often *at least* twenty to thirty years old before they bear any fruit. So, too, stories take time. And if we know anything about the power of autumn, we know that leaves drop off the trees because a new bud is tenderly showing up. So as we let go of beliefs, new ones quietly appear, giving us room to grow and become all over again as we send the fruit and seeds on to future generations. As we think about our beliefs, let's consider a short practice for how we change and how we can let go.

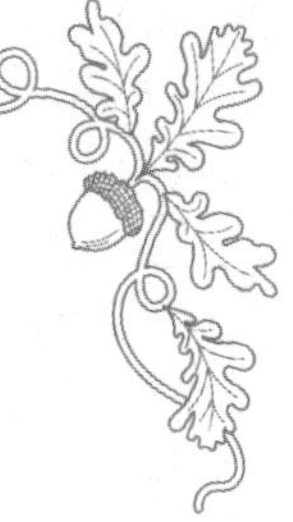

Practice for Letting Go of Old Beliefs and Opening Up to the Childlike Curiosity of New Beliefs

Light a candle.

Take four deep breaths to the four directions.

Name or write down one belief you've held that causes harm to yourself or to others or to the earth.

Allow your body to tense up for ten seconds, and then release the tension. As your body relaxes, release the belief.

Repeat the process for up to five beliefs you've held.

Pause and pay attention to the ways these beliefs have harmed you and others.

Release the grief or shame you may feel and embrace love.

Take four deep breaths to the four seasons of life.

Now name or write down a belief that you've picked up, one rooted in love and care.

Hold your hands palms up, and allow a soft smile to ease onto your face for ten seconds.

Repeat the process for up to five new beliefs.

Put your hands to your heart and thank your child self for journeying alongside you.

Take four more deep breaths.

Hold a moment of gratitude for your journey and everywhere it's taken you.

Blow out the candle.

After this practice, ask yourself if you have space for the deeper process of making amends when it comes to belief systems that have harmed others. We cannot change who we've been in the past, but we can reach out to those who have been hurt by our actions based on those beliefs. We can rewrite the story with compassion and care and see what happens.

Finally, let's consider our beliefs and our relationship with Mother Earth. One of the most powerful ways we challenge a story is through the art we consume, and in so many ways, we come back to our relationship with the earth again and again through art.

In 2024, I wrote a summer series called "Mother Earth Practices for Summer" for my Substack community at *The Liminality Journal*, and one of the practices, a piece called "Mother Earth-Driven Politics," focused on the idea that our relationship with Mother Earth drives our politics and beliefs, not the other way around. I wrote:

> Think about the way colonization has worked throughout the centuries, separating peoples from the land, desecrating Mother Earth, destroying waters, trees, and the peoples who care for them.
>
> It's important to separate our souls and bodies from Mother Earth for colonialism and authoritarianism to thrive.
>
> So, how do we remain connected? We have to remember that our relationship to the earth is the thing that drives us in life.
>
> So when we are disconnected, severed, hurting, we play that out in relationships, politics, social circles, all of it.
>
> And when we begin to heal, when we practice care, comfort, connection with Segmekwe, we begin to live *differently*. It shows up in every aspect of our lives.
>
> So, whether we want to admit it or not, our connection to the living beings around us, to Earth, our Mother, absolutely matters in the world we find ourselves navigating today.[6]

Most importantly, there is no solution to war, hate, genocide, climate collapse, or democracy collapse without relationship to Mother Earth, without acknowledging that we belong to her, that we have a connection to heal. We need to acknowledge the severed connection, to pay attention to the ways our beliefs must change when it comes to the earth. When we begin to do that, things around the world can change, *must change*. A new story can be told and restored from an older one, renewed for future generations, one community at a time. How beautiful.

One community that is shifting the way they connect to Mother Earth is the Shipibo people of the Peruvian Amazon as new generations rise up to protect the lands and trees around them from loggers, colonizers, and palm plantations. In 2023, Jeremy Seifert and Fred Bahnson released a short film called *The Forest Beyond* about Senen Kaisi, a young woman who travels to the edges of the rainforest to understand more of what's happening on her ancestral homelands and find ways to respond. One of the most powerful moments happens when Senen connects with an elder, Sanken Kena, who takes her to the rainforest after Senen shares that she has never seen the trees, never touched them, never connected with them, only heard stories from her grandmother.

While in the rainforest, Sanken Kena shares, "Here there is everything. . . . There are medicinal plants that cure us," as she points out the caru caru trees, which are being extracted from the forests alongside the mahogany trees and all the creatures who call those trees their homes. Senen looks around in awe and says, "I've lived in the Amazon my whole life and I've never known an immense forest like this until today." This young woman, whose community has been completely deforested, looks up in awe at the strength and height of the mahogany tree, with what I'm sure is a mix of joy, kinship, and immense grief.

As she returns home ready to fight for the lands of her ancestors, she says, "I'll tell my family to watch over the forest and live in peace."[7]

What would it mean for us to watch over the lands and waters and to live in peace? The next time you're in the presence of trees, take a moment to thank them for their kinship and generosity. Let your care for them become an everyday commitment, not just for a healthier, cleaner earth but to foster a relationship *with* them, *with* this earth that has loved us since time began.

When it comes to our relationship with Mother Earth, all of us, *all of us*, continue to claw and pray and fight and create our way through the vicious and deadly grips of colonialism, and we find our rainforests and our elders and our precious stories in the midst of all of it as we journey to change ourselves and to change the world as we know it. We draw on the hope of future generations and the sustainable power of stories to get us there.

At the dawn, Grandmother Moon and
Grandfather Sun pass by each other,
and I imagine their interactions—
a quick wink, a head nod that says,
"We've kept this tender world
together another night," or
"Don't forget to clock out and
enjoy some rest," and they laugh
because time and rest are small ideas
in their grand, kind power.
Maybe Grandfather Sun says,
"You looked beautiful up there,"
and Grandmother Moon blushes
as she takes a bouquet of starlight
with her into the coming day.

DROPPING SEEDS

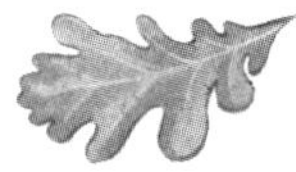

Stories are received as treasured gifts to be held in our hearts, and the recipient has a responsibility to share them with those who may need them.

—Jennifer Grenz, *Medicine Wheel for the Planet*

Compost and New Birth for Future Generations

One day, Story passes on, and as they do,
the fruits of their life are felt and shared
by all who knew them,
by those who read about them
and understood the deep love that they were formed in
and the deep love they passed to everyone they met.
Story lived a life of joy and connection
and passed that on for everyone who came after them,
a true legacy of love, care, and connection.

17

INTERFAITH, EXPANSIVE, FUTURISTIC STORIES

We've entered the stage of the life of a story when we witness endings as beginnings, when we ask what happens after someone has lived a full life. What happens beyond being an elder? What do we pass on to future generations? Which seed-stories do we want to grow and flourish in the future, and which ones should we allow to rest?

Here is the complicated, difficult, beautiful thing I have to tell you as we come to the last part of this book: Stories never really die. They become compost, moving from one kind of existence to another, transforming from one form to a different one, given back to the earth, picked up by an animal or person to become something else, all while never fully going away.

In *We Survived the End of the World,* Chickasaw author Steven Charleston explores apocalyptic stories of prophecy or revelation and reminds us of the importance of this moment we are living in, a moment marked by liminality, a moment of deep clarity and transition, deep fears, and big questions. Simultaneously, Charleston's book reminds us of the opportunity to dream and come together to ask what our stories mean and where they are headed. We remember the intergenerational Indigenous wisdom that brings us here, to this moment: "Pandemics, environmental destruction, corrupt governments, war, and natural disasters: my ancestors have been through it all before. They have survived, and they have returned to the land of the living. They bring a message of hope and transformation. They offer a vision of healing and restoration. They have something to tell us about how apocalypse works."[1]

This is the way life works, as our stories cycle and revolve around and around one another: We look to our ancestors and remember who we are; we live our lives for future generations, for healing that ripples across timelines and our limited understanding; and we do it all through our sacred connection to the lands and waters around us. Indigenous futures are essential to the stories we tell, to the gifts we choose to give to those who come after us. Our stories can be, *must be*, expansive and future-looking as we acknowledge everything we've come through to get to this moment.

In 2024, *National Geographic* released a special print issue called "Indigenous Futures," focusing on global Indigenous realities and hopes for the future. The issue covered former Secretary of the Interior Deb Haaland and her work with communities, Aboriginal women in the Wet Tropics of Queensland working with controlled fires, a Quechua rapper named Cay Sur whose art is used to honor protest and survival, Yoruba creative Ayo Lawson connecting with her Indigenous ancestry by celebrating queerness in filmmaking, and guardians watching over Cofan land in Ecuador.

In a powerful article titled "A Future in Indigenous Hands," *National Geographic* explorer Keolu Fox shares, "Charting this

Indigenous future—shifting our consciousness—will mean adopting a shared vision where the wisdom of the past guides us for generations to come. One where technology serves humanity's deepest values and aspirations. Where the guardianship of the Earth and the equitable distribution of its resources defines progress."[2]

How can we take better responsibility for our stories—the stories we keep, the ones we pass around like a plague, the ones we hold on to for dear life because we can't let them go, stories of dangerous nostalgia, stories that might keep us trapped in things like grief and anger, stories of love and compassion? How can we be better caretakers?

Can we hold the everlasting nuance and complexity that come with stories?

Without feeling like the world is completely falling apart around us, can we ask what stories mean to us and be honest about how we have twisted and manipulated them, about how we have built a world of stifling pain as well as a world of solid joy?

Even as I was writing this book, the world was showing itself to be a difficult place, and people were showing themselves to be capable of incredible hatred. We witnessed ongoing violence in Palestine and Ukraine. There was gang violence in Haiti, atrocities in Congo, mass starvation in Sudan, horrific flooding in Appalachia, and wildfires across the world that destroyed homes and lives. In Arariboia, Indigenous guardians continued fighting to save the rainforests of Brazil from deforestation and destruction.

The daily, weekly, monthly struggle to write this book always came with the question of whether I could. Could I block out everything happening and find the energy to write these words? Could I pay attention to the world but also make sure I cared for myself enough to get this book to your hands? Could I balance it all?

The beauty and terror of being a writer means we have to sit in the reality of all of it, but sometimes I doubt the work of alchemy to take the pain and transform it into something I can give to you. And once I do give it to you, will it help? Will it be a balm for the pain or a deeper reminder of it? Will my words bring healing, or have I missed something? Are my stories too warped to be trusted?

Then one day in May 2024 while writing and grieving and feeling so incredibly hopeless about everything going on in the world, I reminded myself of the way stories work. Stories are liminal, complex, nuanced, full of joy and pain, love and hatred. It's hard to place stories into just one category, hard to make them one thing or another. Stories are complex because people are, *because the world is.*

From the miracle of an acorn growing into a sapling, to the aged rings and deeply grounded roots, oak trees are a picture of what it means to live a complex, ever-forming life. The life cycle of an oak tree reminds us of how powerful life can be—that it's heartbreaking, beautiful, honest, and true.

I realized that I can live in that complexity as I write—in fact, I have to. I *have to* exist in the liminal space of war and poverty, of things not being as they should be yet. I can exist in the truth that words themselves bring hope; they keep us alive and moving, living and breathing, even in the midst of war and famine and genocide and colonialism. We don't check out of the world in order to write. We write our way through the heavy world in hopes that we help make it a better one.

I think of this quote from Eboo Patel's book *We Need to Build*: "Looking for the bad in everything means that you ignore the good, and you absolve yourself of any responsibility for building things that are better."[3] Patel writes with such deep and enduring hope, because even interfaith conversations can be riddled with hate, frustration, and anger. He reminds us of who we can be and who we are, the liminal parts of us that long for healing and care. As we pay attention to the hurting world and the brokenness in it, we also look ahead, around us, asking what stories we are ready to carry forward to future generations.

The roots of an oak tree express community and care, which is interesting as we get to the maturity of the tree and pay attention to this season of dropping acorns once again. What happens beneath the surface? The oaks show us that though they are independent in body, they deeply care about one another, protect one another, intertwine themselves with the others around them for safekeeping.

As we watch the way our stories grow, we see that our rootedness is where care and kindness happen, where community comes to call.

When we look even deeper into the tree, we see the rings that create a tree's inner world. The rings of a tree represent history; they represent every acorn that grew into a sapling, every moment that tree was tended to as it grew to maturity. Every ring, I believe, has a memory. The rings are a story within a story within a story, fully and deeply embodied. Sara Gurulé, who is of Apache, Spanish, and Basque descent, wrote a piece for the Coalition to Dismantle the Doctrine of Discovery about the rings of trees and what they teach her about colonization, storytelling, and land: "Tree rings overall are the tree's life story embodied—with tremendous effort and for the sake of growing and living, the tree creates a beautiful and unique story with its very being. The Tree People teach me about storytelling in this way. As ancient witnesses—such as my favorite tree, the bristlecone pine—they teach us that the acts of storytelling, story sharing, and story keeping are sacred acts."[4]

The futuristic hope of storytelling means we pay attention. It means we pause and ask what the tree rings of the world teach us about our history, about where we've come from, about the landscape we leave behind, because we cannot build a better world until we've come to terms with the one we've already built.

In my book *Living Resistance*, I write that I believe in Us, by which I mean the collective *Us*, the *Us* that we cannot escape.[5] A tree cannot escape their roots, cannot change their inner rings—and we cannot escape ours.

Sacred Imagining Exercise for Future Generations

Close your eyes and take four deep breaths to the four directions.

Now, begin to imagine.

When you hear words like *care*, *kinship*, *belonging*, what do you imagine? What is the landscape you see before you? Who is there, and what are they doing? What does belonging feel like?

Repeat this word over and over—*belonging, belonging, belonging*—and let it sink into your body.

We use our sacred imaginations to dream, to draw on a future world and future generations who are reaching back to us right now, right this moment. Imagine you are reaching out your hands to them, holding on to them, to this dream of yours.

Like you're pulling on a rope in tug-of-war, pull the dream and future generations closer, closer to you, just for a moment.

Take a few deep breaths as you pull them close.

Tell them what you want them to hear, a message you want to send to them. Tell them that we are passing on stories of love and hope.

Receive their love in return.

Then send them off with love and care.

Place your hands over your heart, bringing this intergenerational love into every aspect of your being.

Take a few deep breaths.

Open your eyes.

When I think about the expansive ways we dream of the future, I think of what I call a "bubble of expansion." I can remember numerous times, seasons, moments in my life, and snapshots that I now see as my bubble expanding. Growing up Southern Baptist, I lived in a very particular bubble, where anyone outside that bubble, anyone "other," was considered a threat and a danger to our existence as Christians.

Then I grew up. I left my hometown. I studied social work and world literature. I met new people, and slowly, ever so slowly, my bubble began to expand, to include those I was once told to be afraid of. My bubble expanded as my beliefs and ways of understanding the world and myself kept expanding, as I met new people from different faiths, cultures, ethnicities, backgrounds. My world is better because of those moments; my work as a writer is richer because of those people.

In 2023, I took part in a project with the Aspen Institute and the Bahá'ís of the United States called The Narratives of America Project. A group of us contributed essays to a publication, of the same title, and in the summer of 2024 we gathered in DC at the Aspen Institute to celebrate the launch of the publication.

We were there, a group of diverse folks—diverse racially, ethnically, religiously, culturally—coming together to ask what kind of future we hope for America, what community is supposed to look like, what embodiment and justice are. I spoke first at the gathering, sharing my thoughts on that future, specifically my hopes for the creative prophets who will rise up and show us the way back to our humanity, who will remind us that we live in a liminal space between those who came before us and those who will come after us.

Envisioning the future requires imagination, and it takes time—time in prayer and thought and, yes, in community. We need to step back and ask who our community is and how we are showing up with them. I think of some of the authors I'm in virtual and soul community with, those who are trying to instill healing and care in a hurting world, who encourage me to do the same. This work of kinship and solidarity requires us to lean into these liminal spaces where we connect with one another, where we dream and ask big questions together, not just to get answers but because the work of asking in community *creates* community.

When we envision a new narrative for America, the impact is huge. Who and what are we imagining for the future? Who is there, how did they get there, and what are they doing? In this, our stories become futuristic and full of hope. They bring us closer to one another as we build the future through our words, our art, our passions, our gifts, our work. And when the world is chaotic and heavy, when we feel the rise of hate, we hold each other and that future dream close and let it guide us every single day.

When we ask how our stories can be intercultural, interspiritual, guiding us toward future generations, I think of the seven grandfather teachings as a guide for us moving forward. The beauty of our Indigenous teachings is that the stories we've learned are ancient, surviving year after year, act of colonization after act of colonization. Our stories are ancient, but they are also modern. They are of our ancestors but also for all future generations. We, and our stories, are still here—and we will always be here.

Turtle Mountain descendant and language teacher James Vukelich Kaagegaabaw writes about the seven grandfather teachings (humility, bravery, honesty, wisdom, truth, love, and respect) and shares that they remind him of various spiritual teachings from around the world, including from Buddhism, Hinduism, Jainism, and the Christian New Testament.[6] This shows us again that, like the roots of many oak trees, our beliefs, our future hopes, and our dedication to peace and care in the world are connected. The more we practice care for and grow this bond, the more difficult it will be to break.

There are lands I have just met who seem to know my name.
When I whispered hello, they whispered back, a breath
of recognition and space. "You are here," they spoke,
as tears of familiarity filled my eyes. "You are not of us,
but you are us," they claimed as the wind rustled
the hawthorn leaves above my head.
We seem to think that, as weary wanderers, we bring ourselves
to a place—every story carried in our suitcase.
But, it seems, the places we wander to already knew we
were coming, our stories already carried on the ocean breeze
before we found our way to its shores.
If Eagle can carry our prayers to God, Eagle can carry
our wonders and wounds to the clouds, the grass, the waters.
So, next time, don't say hello.
Say, "I'm here," or "Look at you, you're beautiful," or
"Dear friend, it's me," as if only time has kept you apart.
Controlled time is an hourglass that is about to be shattered.

18

MERGING STORIES

Every year in May, we do something at *The Liminality Journal* called "A Poem a Day in the Month of May," in which we write daily poems based on one-word prompts that I send out connected to some macro theme for the month.

In 2024, the theme was "Words Are Hope," because we were desperately trying to make sense of a world that was desperately trying to figure out who it was. We were questioning democracies, calling out governments and institutions that upheld war machines and genocide, and watching protestors across the United States (and in many other parts of the world) demand peace.

When we pause and ask what kind of stories we want to continue on in the world, I think about empathy, about how stories come alive when we are placed in each other's lives, when we, as the saying goes, take a walk in another's shoes. It's true, isn't it? I didn't understand my atheist friends because I knew only the Southern Baptist bubble I'd grown up in. I was told being gay is a sin, but then I met gay friends and professors in college and realized how beautiful and expansive love truly is and how much harm is caused by the toxic and deadly stories we tell and act on.

Do you see? Our empathy is born in stretching ourselves beyond the toxic bubbles and boundaries we place within our communities, institutions, and nations. When we expand outside those bubbles, when we step into the world and our confirmation bias is challenged, we have the opportunity to be stretched.

On May 4, 2024, our one-word prompt was *empathy*, and below is a section from the poem I wrote:

> I do not wish to burn out
> my precious light of empathy,
> but to hold it gently, just like I wish
> to hold the hearts of my neighbors,
> of kids dying across the world
> and loved ones crying out
> for every loved one they've lost.
>
> I wish for an empathy that endures
> through the seven generations,
> that keeps us connected at our
> heart centers because we should be,
> because it matters, because our world
> needs us to remember
> that once you walk in another's shoes
> for long enough, you feel the callouses
> and scars that make up an entire life.
>
> Let me put it plainly:
>
> I want to put down the shame
> and put on the shoes,
> and slowly, quietly,
> hands entwined,
> candles lit in unity,
> walk my neighbor home.[1]

We must show up to our empathy, to our work in the world, with a clear vision. This is why I end my book *Living Resistance* with the importance of sustainability, and that includes our dreams, the vision of what we work toward. Our resistance to a dangerous and toxic status quo in the world won't do anything if we don't make the work sustainable, if we don't embody it for future generations to carry on tending to the seeds we are planting right here, right now: "Dreams are so powerful—both our literal dreams, the dreams we have at night while we are sleeping, and the daydreaming that keeps us moving forward in our waking hours. Dreams are intergenerational and stretch across cultures, faiths, and beliefs. Dreams carry us."[2]

In order to have empathy for others, and even to have empathy for future generations whose lives we can only imagine, we need to be settled and grounded in who we are, in what our dreams and visions are for this world. What is the work that you are called to do in the world? What makes you come alive? As you discover what makes you come alive, you'll hold space for others to share what it is that makes them come alive. In this exchange of ideas, hopes, and dreams, we find empathy and kinship, a merging and blending of lives that produces beautiful fruit.

These are the acorns that are falling from mature oak elder to the ground, taking root slowly, and starting the whole process of rebirth and renewal over again. These are the stories that are reborn again and again, and as they grow, they merge, just like the thousands of acorns that cover the ground of a forest merge to become the trees that shelter and hold them. We can't rush the process, and we can't underestimate the importance of what happens when stories merge, when our stories come together and are forced to look each other in the eyes to make sense of everything.

What happens when we face the world of stories that we've been given? My friend Dr. Pooja Lakshmin asks, When the systems are broken, what do we do with the stories? She writes in *Real Self-Care*, "Burning it all down—whether it's your life or the system—doesn't fix the problem. It's just another way of running from your problems, only to find them staring back at you in the mirror. To truly change the system, we must work from the inside out, starting right where we are—in our current lives."[3]

Instead of talking about burning it all down, we ask what it means to merge, to come together and pave the way for the future. This is what happened for wildlife ecologist and TV host Dr. Rae Wynn-Grant, who writes in her book *Wild Life* about how her own stories merged when she challenged what she'd been told, that Black women couldn't be scientists and didn't belong in the outdoors: "For my entire life, I'd felt that I didn't have a place in nature, in the wilderness, that it was unavailable to me. I didn't see people who looked like me—whether a Black person, woman, or a Black woman—represented as being stewards of the environment, being confident in and down and dirty with nature."[4]

She allowed these stories—of being a Black adventurer and being a woman—to merge in her life, and because of it, she became part of a movement and culture to show the world that Black women can be wildlife ecologists and host their own television shows, that they can show up in the spaces that bring passion to their lives.

Prentis Hemphill writes about the importance of dreaming in *What It Takes to Heal*: "We commit to our own healing in part because the realization of what we are dreaming of rests on it. It is our responsibility to one another to do our internal work, not so that we feel good alone but to stay an active part of the whole to refuse to pass down to the next generation what pain we've accrued."[5] Dreaming is about what we give the future, a merging of stories from the now and from the future—the stories we are helping carry forward.

Leah Lakshmi Piepzna-Samarasinha writes about the power of science fiction in *The Future Is Disabled*: "Science fiction is full of disabled writers and writers writing disability, both those who claim the D-word publicly and those who don't—or aren't—but who consistently write worlds that go beyond disability as tragedy or nonexistent, where disabled main characters live within and transform apocalypse out of their disabled genius and guts."[6] When we gather courage to allow our stories to merge, to bring into focus things that we'd rather ignore, we are giving life to better stories. We are choosing to connect to the future in new ways. We are rejecting the status quo of hate, ableism, sexism, colonialism in our stories, in our words, in our very bodies.

When traveling on long flights, I find that, about halfway through, my eyes get dry and an anxious feeling rises in my chest as I observe the countless screens around me, mounted to the seats or held in the hands of passengers. There is no escape from experiencing stories as they stream, all at once, too many for my system to handle. Even now, while on a flight, I see *The SpongeBob SquarePants Movie* to my left, a horror film to my right, and *Gilmore Girls* a few rows up. Overwhelmed, I close my eyes and take my spirit somewhere else, somewhere safe, where my senses are calmed again.

We're not made for this, for a bombardment of stories. We already carry many within us, and that's true magic, I believe. But at some point, we hit our threshold, too full to focus, too overwhelmed to make sense of things. I feel similarly when I scroll through social media, coming across story after story, reel after reel, searching for the healing I so desperately need. Instead of taking in these stories in excess or altogether escaping them, we need to learn to sift through what we're experiencing in order to embrace and alchemize the stories within us and around us.

In the fall of 2024, when I traveled to Northern Ireland to help facilitate a retreat on storytelling and healing, I discovered the power of merging stories, of asking questions of the stories we encounter and learning which stories to embrace when there are so many important ones out in the world. It is nearly impossible to ignore the power of stories when pondering the histories and present-day realities of Northern Ireland. While there, I encountered the stories of granite stones from the mountains of the Kingdom of Mourne and stories of farmers' everyday lives among the green hills. I bore witness to the stories of East and West Belfast and the ways that they imagine peacemaking and progress between groups of people with different beliefs, between Catholic and Protestant, fighting the realities and language of "othering" every single day. The people are showing up to peacemaking in a heavy and violent world. I witnessed stories of love and kinship from the garden of a new friend's house, stories told along the path of his homemade labyrinth in the garden. I didn't just bring my stories to Northern Ireland; the stories found me, inviting me into their realities and showing me what could be—how stories of hope can form from the merging stories of the past and the present.

One night at the retreat, I asked all of us what it means to hold space—with ourselves, one another, and Mother Earth. What does kinship mean, and how do we rebuild a society where kinship has been fractured? That night, we took strings of twine and stretched them across the circle our bodies made in the small dining room, and one by one I cut the strings, reminding us that as much as we have connected, we have also fractured our connections. Then we found new partners and tied those severed strings back together, an image that shows us healing is possible, our grief and our joy can merge, and that the scars that are left will tell us a story of healing. On this trip, I was introduced to the Irish drum, the bodhran, a traditional Celtic instrument edged with wood and covered in goat skin. I noticed one in the back of my friend Terry's car. When I asked about it, he explained to me that the sound of the drum is like the sound that comes from our gut, our spirit. I smiled and immediately told him about the traditional drums in my Anishinaabe culture, that the steady beat we dance to in ceremony represents a mother's heartbeat.

The gut and the heart are two sacred places where stories live and merge—where they alchemize, where they become a driving force for our lives—where we learn what it means to safely reclaim the sacredness of our shared imagination for love and peace in the world, again and again. What better way to remember that than through music, through the beat of the drum, through embodiment?

To embrace healing for the future, we have to sit in the liminal spaces, in the sacred—and sometimes scary—spaces where stories meet. We have to be willing to own the difficult stuff and let ourselves move through it, on our own *and* in community. This is what has happened in Northern Ireland, through years and years of peace talks between differing political, religious, and social groups, peace talks held both in secret and in public, peace talks that asked what the gut and the heart need for all peoples in a society to thrive. There are still scars and wounds, but healing can still happen, and we can all learn from their stories. When we live by our hearts, we learn to look beyond the binaries we have set up in society. When we live by our guts, we trust the journey of opening up when we want to stay closed off. Interaction brings healing to our stories, merging the past with the present, helping us move beyond othering and into belonging.

While on my trip, I read about Saint Brigid of Kildare through John Philip Newell. Brigid is a beloved Celtic goddess and Christian saint across Ireland, a woman said to have been born on the threshold between night and day, who holds the tender mystery of Celtic Christianity in her bones, who fiercely brought together her own spirituality and a constant groundedness with and care for Mother Earth, helping others to do the same. She is a healer and a midwife and helps us, even today, give birth to a new vision of tomorrow.

Newell, in his book *Sacred Earth, Sacred Soul*, writes of Brigid, "Who was this beautiful, wild woman? We need the sacred feminine to be strong again within us, not just in women but also in men, and not just in our individual lives but collectively among us in our communities and nations. . . . This is not a strength that is used against another, but for one another."[7] Once again, we see a sacred vision of merging—of meeting one another, of communities collectively passing along stories that bring healing, care, and change to this world. We are called to this—and it calls to us, just as the lands and waters do. The most beautiful thing about all of this is that we can show up exactly as we are to the magic of this work, and we will be welcomed at the table.

When I returned home from the retreat, I wrestled lovingly with my own stories, with the merging of who I am and who I hope to one day be. In this wrestling, the realities of Jesus and Saint Brigid, of my own roots of paganism and Christianity, of Celtic and Indigenous joy in the world, showed up in this poem, and I'd like to share it with anyone who is feeling a sacred, exhausting, beautiful merging in their own life that will lead to a transformed future.

> I'd like to sit down
> to a long lunch with
> Saint Brigid of Ireland
> and Jesus of Bethlehem
> and have a conversation
> about liminality.
>
> I'd like to know about
> that water to wine situation
> and what it means to rest,
> how it feels to wander

hillsides tending to people's
deepest needs.

I'd love to understand
how to bring people
together at water wells
of healing when everyone
says we are better apart.

I hope they'd ask me
how I can be quiet yet
full of fire, and what it means
for each of us to have lived
in the time we lived in, what
it means to show up liminally
in a world that doubts the
power of paradox.

I'd like us all to tell our favorite
stories of Mother Earth and
remember the cultures we
come from and the ones we
constantly return to, the
ones that hold us even when
we forget ourselves.

I'd like us to grieve the things
that aren't as they should be:
colonialism and genocide,
oppression and hate, and,
right then and there, hold each
other's hands and promise to
never give up on the power of
kinship and belonging.

Then I'd like us to finish
our cups of coffee, brush
the dust from our shoulders,
and vow to meet again in
the Otherworld, the Milky Way,
in the highest heavens,
so we can look around together
at every moment when the
people found each other's
sacred centers and decided
to get it right.

19

STORIES FOR HEALING

The power of a story is in the telling, right? How we tell a story creates the story's narrative, helps decide where the characters will live, who they will live with, how they will interact with those around them. How we label stories matters too.

In the newest *Doctor Who* series on Disney+, we come to the final episode, the culmination of the relationship between Ruby and the Doctor, and the great mystery of Ruby's mother. But my favorite, favorite thing about the ending (spoiler alert for anyone who hasn't watched it yet—stop here and skip the next two paragraphs if you plan to!) is that Ruby's mother was not magical or mighty but absolutely, beautifully, perfectly *ordinary*.

The Doctor lovingly holds Ruby close and explains, "In the end, the most important person in the universe was the most ordinary—a scared little girl making her baby safe."[1]

I'm brought to tears fairly easily by a good story, but this line really undid me, because it's so true in so much of life that the ordinary, the small, the *tiny acorns in their tiny shells* are the things that change everything, alter history, and shape or reshape the whole world. Ruby's mom was an ordinary young mother, and her ordinariness overcame one of the greatest evils that the universe had ever known.

For my thirty-fifth birthday, I asked for a composter, and you should have seen my joy in putting it together in the living room, the miracle that each panel truly fit with the next. I marveled over that the first bowl of eggshells and fruit scraps mixed with browns from the lawn that would be, over time, transformed to feed our garden.

I could take you down the path of worms and what they do for compost, but in my composter, we don't use worms. Instead, we rely on the air, the rotation of the bins, and the creatures—gnats, flies, and bugs that find their way in and slowly, slowly over time break down our food to become this incredibly rich addition to our soil. Those food scraps and their creature kin find their way back to their origins, dirt to dirt, land back to land, again and again.

It is a community practice, all of us together, making compost happen. Because compost isn't just the eggshells that I put into a big plastic bin that I spin around in my yard. It's also the dead leaves and the unused acorns that fall from the tops of the oak tree down to the ground, layer upon layer upon layer that pile up slowly, slowly over time and become the humus in the soil that helps new plants grow.

So, too, some of our stories fall to the ground or quietly fade away into the ether to become part of our air, our atmosphere, always there but making their way back to dust again. How can we be good stewards of this part of the process, of the composting part? Can our outdated and problematic stories become compost for new stories to grow? This is one of the surest paths to healing, honoring which stories we can and should hold on to that foster love in the world and which ones to let go of. As we grow older alongside our stories, it is our responsibility to pay attention to how healing should happen.

How do we imagine our relationship to stories as the world goes on, as history continues to live on, as we ask what future generations need from us?

Daje James, a.k.a. The Story Doula, is a brand strategist, author, and artist who helps people investigate their stories and ask how they show up with their energy in the world. I love the ideas that James embodies, helping us see stories—individually and collectively—in new ways, noticing the openings all around us, invitations to new horizons that expand our thinking and imaginations and build a new world. Stories live in online spaces. They live in offline spaces. They live where we put our words and our energy, because energy is expansive.

What exactly is a doula, and what does being a doula have to do with storytelling? A doula is a nonmedical companion who supports a woman physically and emotionally throughout childbirth, so we can imagine that being a story doula is about being a companion to a story and also the one who bears witness to the birth and life of that story.

James Hogue was a doula for his wife, Shunquita, a few years ago and then started his organization called Fathers Assisting Mothers, which offers a bootcamp for men to become doulas for their partners or other birthing folks in their lives. What a beautiful gift, a way to stretch and name and expand a status quo story—one that for so long told of only women in the birthing room, only women as nurses and doulas. When we break through stories and imagine something new, we change things for future generations, and that is exactly what Hogue is doing. Being a doula is incredibly powerful, a kind of supportive partnership that we need more of in this world—and in our stories.

There are also death doulas, those who accompany others as they pass from this life to another one. Alua Arthur writes beautifully and authentically about becoming a death doula in her book *Briefly Perfectly Human*: "The idea of death is a seed. When that seed is carefully tended, life grows like wildflowers in its place.

The only thing in our control is how we choose to engage with our mortality once we become aware of it."[2]

The idea of death is a seed, it's a story, a story we choose to tend to, choose to let grow—just as we grow. This is such a beautiful image as we embrace the stories around us and as we ask what stories we are leaving for future generations. What a gift for future generations that we get the chance to approach life and death with care, with nuance, and yes, even with some joy. We get to explore what it means to accompany stories through life *and through death,* through every single season we encounter.

So, how are we story doulas? We tenderly and strongly hold on to narratives with others in kinship and solidarity. As story doulas, we support others as they navigate stories, as they navigate the very real aspects of life. Maybe your therapist is your story doula. Maybe it's your best friend. Maybe the elder down the street is your doula. Maybe you are your own story doula—I know I've taken on this role over the last few years as I've begun healing the relationship to my child self. How can I heal the story between Little Me and Current Me, and how can I help others do the same?

In 2023, I was a guest on Glennon Doyle's podcast *We Can Do Hard Things,* and we talked about five ways to be more present, including connecting to our child selves and to Mother Earth through our bodies. I shared about how, growing up, I learned to balance a checkbook but not how to care for my relationship with the earth. I still remember sitting in Mr. Zumwalt's class realizing that filling out a check is one of the hallmarks of being an adult. But what else matters? Our curiosity? Our sense of adventure? Our childlike wonder? Humility? In essence, we can *live* a different story about our bodies in connection to earth, our Mother. So many listeners shared what it meant to begin reframing this relationship to the world around us and to her as a being, to find ways to put an old story in the compost bin and let it become a nutrient for future generations. In that way, we are actually proclaiming that there is some redemption in those toxic stories that can return to the dust and find their way home again. It's mystical, it's magical, and it's beautiful.

In being a story doula, we must face the life cycle of a story, just like we watch the life cycle of an oak tree come full circle. When acorns fall from an elder tree, they lay dormant for a while, for an entire season, sometimes for a few years, sometimes forever.

I want to share portions of something I wrote in my personal journal about the process of tending to my own stories of healing when it comes to my relationship with the world around me and trusting my own guidance.

> In 2023, I bought a book of fifty hikes in Pennsylvania at a local thrift store. We'd lived in the Philadelphia area for about three years, and I wanted not just to get to know our state but to do so by walking the land and getting to know the stories that are told only on a hiking trail.
>
> The thing is that no one gives us a guidebook as storytellers. We step into storytelling, or we are brought in by our elders, our teachers, our kin. Storytelling is passed through our mouths, our words, our spirits exchanging something sacred we often can't explain.
>
> No one gives us a guidebook for how to grieve, or how to face our fears, or how to stop judging ourselves and others all the time. I bought a book at an REI in Madison, Wisconsin, while I was visiting for a speaking event a few years ago. It's a guided journal for women who are finding their way to the outdoors. I get a little embarrassed every time I open it, like I'm not allowed to, like I won't live up to the expectations of the book itself, like I'm not ready to dream. That, too, is a toxic story I tell myself.
>
> The difficult thing about stories is that we aren't always prepared for the landscape. We don't always know what to do when stories intersect, when they diverge, when they contradict or cause us pain or harm. What do we do with those stories? Who wrote the guidebook for them, to help us make sense of what a story is supposed to feel like, look like, sound like?

> So, I bought that book of Pennsylvania hikes because I'm learning to hike. And I write books, maybe so that they can become guidebooks themselves—guidebooks on how to be human, on what mistakes feel like, on how the earth holds us steady all the time. . . .
>
> What does it mean to experience stories in a visceral way? When I'm hiking, that's all there is—a visceral awareness of my anxiety, the sacred world, my innate curiosity, my fear, my childlike joy, all of it. There's no guidebook for that either, but we keep going, because that's where we write our own guidebook, where we become our own teachers, where we realize that all this time we've been tethered to Mother Earth in unimaginable ways and that she, too, has been speaking stories over us.
>
> As we pay attention to the work of storytelling, as we build our own guidebook for it, how do we pay attention to what a story needs along the way? If we are story doulas, we are also life and death doulas. We are doulas for the liminal spaces, for the parts of life no one wants to talk about or acknowledge, along the rocky paths and hikes we don't quite understand yet.

The really hard part is when a story ends—when we realize the American dream isn't what we thought it was, or the people we trusted didn't treat us well, or we peel back layers of greed in the spaces around us. When this happens, we grieve. Grief is part of the process of stories being composted, so accompanying one another through that grief is part of our work.

My friend J.S. Park, a fellow author and chaplain, has a gorgeous, honest book on grief called *As Long as You Need*. He writes, "We survive the nightmare of loss, I think, by dreaming. To dream is to cope. . . . The world continues to be cruel and unfair, but we dream amid the wreckage of what no longer is."[3]

We can, and perhaps must, journey with grief and dreams at the same time. I think it's part of who we are as humans, if we are willing to accept it. That means we choose to tell different stories, to take part in new spaces of community and connection. It means we examine who we've been and who we want to be.

How can we continue to frame storytelling as a living, breathing practice that brings consequences into the world? Future generations are owed that kindness, that of our paying attention or noticing so that when we choose a story, when we help give birth to a story, we do so with intention and care, with kinship in our minds and hearts, so that when a story is returned to the earth, it is done so with care as well.

We also prepare for future generations when we tend to our own roots, our own stories of belonging and care, assessing who we are now and who we hope to be. In other words, just like the mighty oak tree, as we are trimmed back, damaged, hurt, our roots are still there, and our stories "will resprout from the energy contained in the roots."[4]

How are we paying attention to our roots, the roots of our stories, the things that ground us? What energy of love, care, compassion, connection, hate, greed, judgment, and prejudice are we holding on to?

"The chafing and shaping that we allow ourselves to go through and we help others through, that's the only stuff that means anything. These are the things that people consider at their death bed, the only real things."[5] This quote is from a series of videos on YouTube that has become a favorite of mine called *Reflections of Life*. When we work through our stories, seeing them grow and grow and become such an essential part of the world, we are changed by them, and that's pretty powerful. Sometimes as an author and public speaker, I step back and ask not just what I need to write but what will inspire others toward some sort of change, whether it's at the individual or collective level, whether it happens in the micro, mezzo, or macro spaces we inhabit.

But in order for that change to happen, we might have to become a doula—either in the birth of a story or in their transformation back toward the earth they came from.

A Practice for Releasing Stories of Birth and Stories of Death

This is a perfect activity to do when the seasons are changing but especially in autumn as we pay attention to the work of harvest. As the seasons change, the thin veil of time and place lets us know that we are seen and loved.

Take out a sheet of paper and a marker, and draw two large circles, untouching, on the page. Label one circle "letting go" and the other "gathering in."

In the two circles, write what you're letting go of and what you're gathering in for this coming season, for the next few months, for the next few weeks. What are you holding and tending to? What story are you releasing to the sacred compost pile?

Take deep and tender breaths as you work through this. Honor the life you are living, right now. Honor the stories that have been told, the stories that won't be told any longer, the grief that comes with death, the joy that comes with life. Honor all of it in these circles and in this moment.

As humans, we get to hold everything, somehow—the past we've lived, the present we're searching for, the future we've yet to experience but dream will come true. Let's now turn to that future, the future of storytelling, the dreams not yet realized, the stories of love and connection not yet told.

20

THE FUTURE OF STORYTELLING

We're here. We've made it. I know that a book is a linear thing *and* a circular thing, and as always, I hope that this book has felt more like a journey than just a book, more labyrinthine in its complexity and care. I hope you feel like you've arrived at this moment a little different from who you were when you began. I know I'm different here, now, from who I was when I began. Thank you for growing alongside me.

When I got to this point while writing this book, I was incredibly emotional because I realized that I wanted to keep going. There are far too many stories out there waiting to be told, far too many stories that we need to sift through and leave to be composted back to the earth. I didn't want this journey to end because I love stories so, so much, and I know how much we need them in our lives. I know how much you love and need stories too.

My dear friend and Métis storyteller, Chris La Tray, wrote a gorgeous book called *Becoming Little Shell*, and I was drawn to a moment in the book when a number of the folks in the tribe are asking the Little Shell nation who they want to be: "If we believe our ancestors still walk among us, observing with love and curiosity to see what we do next, we must ask ourselves: Who will the Little Shell be? What kind of nation do we want to be? How do we want to show ourselves to the world?"[1]

How do we want to show ourselves to the world? This question should encourage us to ask who we want to be, as tribal nations, as peoples, as humans, as countries, as a collective of storytellers and caretakers. This is where the life of a story has brought us, full circle, asking us what's next.

At one time, the land was a being to be revered and respected. The mountains and valleys, the rocks and waters, these were the greatest storytellers of all time. And then we tried to overtake them, to tell them they didn't matter, that they weren't beings and had no stories to tell. When that happened, we lost something of ourselves, a story of kinship and care severed from our minds and bodies, and we are constantly trying to heal our way back again.

So, what is the future of storytelling? It is about embodiment and care, about what we feel and what we know about being human. I hope that the future of our stories, of the stories out in the world, is a future bound by kinship, connection, and reciprocity, and that means we learn not just how to heal but how to grow together.

Trees are resilient in ways we can barely comprehend. As shared by forest management scholar Wayne Clatterbuck, "Trees do not heal; they seal. . . . After wounding, new wood growing around the wound forms a protective boundary preventing the infection or decay from spreading into the new tissue. Thus, the tree responds to the injury by 'compartmentalizing' or isolating the older, injured tissue with the gradual growth of new, healthy tissue."[2]

As humans with both individual and collective wounds, can we seal off and tend to those wounds in community and kinship? Can we give special care and love to those wounds that have left us hurting for years, maybe centuries, the wounds that have, for so long, taken us away from relationship with one another and Mother Earth? Can we learn to grow new tissue, to tell new stories for future generations?

A few years ago, our family examined the question, What would you do with three wishes? Everyone has different answers to this question based on what they hope for, dream about, or want. My youngest, who was ten years old at the time, wanted a machine that could build LEGO sets, because of course he did—who wouldn't? Then I asked him if there was anything he'd do for others. With three wishes, what would he do for someone else? He paused and admitted that answering that particular question made him feel overwhelmed.

What one wish would change enough things in the world when there are so many problems, so many kinds of oppression, so much hurt and pain? Would we wish everyone had free health care? Would we wish that no one went hungry? Would we wish for an end to all war and militarism? Would we wish that we were just wired differently as humans? My son eventually decided he wished he could take a chunk of the money that today's tech billionaires make in a year and give it away to the people who need it far more than they do, and I couldn't help but nod my head to that one, a nod to Robin Hood and his band of merry men who took what the rich didn't need and gave it to those who did.

What if, instead of three wishes, we had three seeds? What if you had three seeds in the palm of your hand waiting to be planted somewhere, waiting to become stories, to go on their own journey of changing the world?

Close your eyes and picture those seeds for a moment. Three seeds in the palm of your hand.

What do your seeds look like? What shape have they taken? Are they actually acorns, waiting to become mighty oaks, waiting to reorient the whole world toward love?

Now that you've pictured your seeds, ask them who they are. What story are they embodying? What narratives are they shaping? Is one a seed of solidarity and care? Is another seed for every child to find love and joy, or for the end to war and hate? Let them tell you who they are.

Now imagine what you'll do with those seeds. They deserve the best kind of soil, don't they? They deserve to be planted where they will be nourished, where they can grow and become in tenderness, with plenty of light and water and air. Find a place to plant them. Hold this space.

Now, give your energy and care to those seeds, buried deep in the soil. Sing to them, invite them to grow into exactly who they should become, tell them they are beautiful and kind and powerful in the best ways. Bury the reality of these seeds deep in your heart right now. Keep them there. Write them down, type them out, find a space where you'll remember.

There is something incredibly powerful about the collective imagination. It is exactly what's gotten us here, for better or for worse, in all the ways that have led to flourishing and fighting. When we imagine something, we are putting our energy toward it, even if it doesn't happen in our lifetime. When we imagine something, we put words and life toward it, and it matters. So these seeds are our individual and collective imaginings. They are the future we are moving toward, a future that could be, that we want to be, that we desperately hope for.

What seeds have you planted today, and what seeds will you place in the hands of future generations so that they can plant too? In the meantime, while we live our lives, while we go about our daily mundane tasks, we remember those seeds, we tend to them in the deepest parts of us, and we let the ripple effects do exactly what they should do: create a world of embodied, tender, fierce love.

I'll wait for that. Will you?

Something I've learned as I've read stories from oppressed communities around the world is that in the complexity of war, pain, and hate, there are always peacemakers.

Hosna Jalil, who in 2015 was on the president's executive advisory team in Afghanistan, shares that in her work to help women be more self-sufficient, there were always women *and men* who helped her achieve her goals, who helped her fight for human rights and justice.[3] We can drop these stories into the liminal category, because where there is pain and injustice, there are people who show up, surprise us, and help us fight harder for the world we believe in.

Around the world and throughout history, when wars have been waged and peoples have harmed one another again and again, peacekeepers have shown up to ask what it means to tell a better story. Peacekeepers like those in Israel and Palestine have met around tables for years, asking how to embody a more loving story, holding complex conversations and challenging the status quo. They are never the most popular people on social media. They are the liminal space holders. And as the world reminds us how war-torn and painful it can be, we remember them, gathered in cafés and kitchens, hosting Zoom calls, having beautiful and difficult conversations for future generations. When we think we are alone, we look around—really look—and realize that we are far from alone. The world will keep reimagining itself because kinship can truly last even through the most lethal stories.

One of the scariest questions we can ask is, Will the powerful always prevail over the powerless? Will those with more money, influence, and privilege always choose themselves over those with less? There are also those somewhere in the middle, those who can exchange stories, vote in new stories, demand that history be rewritten or that we pay better attention to whose stories are being told. They can disrupt a toxic status quo, hold leaders accountable, partner with others to create change, and there are many of them.

As Howard Thurman teaches, the oppressed are always asking under what conditions survival can occur and remain sustainable while calling out that the status quo is "held by those whose hold on security is sure only as long as the status quo remains intact."[4]

Oh, dear people of the story, do you feel this? *We* are the ones who must pay so much attention, who must lean in and ask where our stories have come from and where they are going. And when we do that with kinship and care at the forefront, we will begin to experience change and cultivate soil that will allow the new story-seeds to grow in the world.

And as those story-seeds grow, we continue to imagine what the future holds, how we hold each other's stories and, in reality, each other's sacredness. We take the stories that we need, grounded in love and belonging, and prepare them for future generations by remembering what we believe about sacredness. "Perhaps we should consider the possibility that the entire reason we have a cognitive impulse to think of God as a divine reflection of ourselves is because we are, every one of us, God. Perhaps rather than concerning ourselves with trying to form a relationship with God, we should instead become fully aware of the relationship that already exists."[5]

I want us to consider these words from Reza Aslan, because they form so much of the root of what we are talking about in this book of stories. Let's see what happens when we replace "God" in this quote with "story": "Perhaps we should consider the possibility that the entire reason we have a cognitive impulse to think of story as a divine reflection of ourselves is because we are, every one of us, story. Perhaps rather than concerning ourselves with trying to form a relationship with story, we should instead become fully aware of the relationship that already exists." We tell stories, we experience stories, but also, we are the stories, and the stories are us, and we live them every single day.

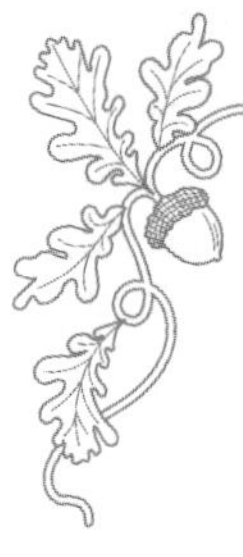

Holding Space as We Go from the Story of Right Now to the Story of Tomorrow

Take four deep breaths to honor the four directions.

Take one more deep breath to honor Mother Earth.

As you close your eyes, imagine that you grab your acorns, the seeds of the stories you want to tell, of love, belonging, warmth, tenderness.

Next, imagine you plant the acorns in nourishing, rich soil. Speak tenderly to them as you do so.

Now, protect those stories—repeat them to those you love, in books, in art, at the dinner table. Each story becomes like a ring of an oak tree; each story grows into its own identity in the world.

Over time, maybe parts of a story don't fit anymore—love becomes more nuanced and secure as it grows—so you thin things out and prune as you need to. You work tenderly.

Belonging truly means *everyone belongs*, so you make sure that the story is told with love and consideration every single time—more pruning, more care.

Then you transplant the story—to new soil, to a new audience, to a bigger space, to a society or a community. Let them grow into the gorgeous, sheltering being that they should have always been. Love grows. Belonging, warmth, and tenderness grow, from person to person, from place to place, until we are all connected, all sheltered.

Again, watch the story grow, watch each branch become a micro-story of the bigger story told, a story that changes the world.

Finally, the story's roots dig deep, deep down into the soil. The story of love connects to the story of kinship, of human rights, of care for Mother Earth. All the stories make a home in this world, soaking up the nourishment of their environment, changing nations and peoples and places forever.

Take a few deep breaths to honor this.

Future generations rest in the shade of these stories, in the tender power of these stories.

Yes.

Let that world come.

Usher it here with every story told, every narrative tended to, for us here and now, for every future generation to come, for every new acorn that falls and asks to grow into a trusted haven for someone else.

The story is alive. Everything is a story.

Sometimes we think
the page has been turned
the portal has been opened
the season has changed
and yet we are still the same,
or so we say when we glance
in the mirror or stare longingly
at a to-do list that won't stop
growing.

But no acorn is surprised to
discover that they will
one day become the oak,
and no butterfly stumbles

from the cocoon wondering
how they got there in the first
place.

Look in the mirror again.
Turn the to-do list into
poetry and let it bring
you deeper into the truth
already waiting to welcome
you back to yourself again,
anew.

The page was always turning,
the portal always opened,
the season already shifting
in and around you the moment
you decided to trust yourself
and make room for The Universe
to steady the path, to transform you,
to weep with joy as you emerged
from where you came bathed in
the light of a new story.

ACKNOWLEDGMENTS

When I think about what an acknowledgment is, I think of those candlelight services that I grew up with in church, the ones where we'd all get those little candles with the cups around them and the paper at the bottom so the wax wouldn't drip onto our hands. Someone would light the candle of the person at the end of each aisle, and then that person would light the next person's candle. Then that person would pass the light to their neighbor as they whispered a word of blessing, and that neighbor would pass the love on to whoever was next to them, and on and on until the whole room was awash with light. There we acknowledged our connectedness, our need to sit in the dark *and* to spark and share the light. That's what these acknowledgments are, me taking my little candle and thanking the others who have kept it lit along the way, who have said *I see you* when I've forgotten to see myself.

Whether we realize it or not, books bring us together with other authors in community. This book was written alongside the authors whose books I read to remember what it means to be a storyteller. I spent my days with them, hours poring over their words and gathering wisdom from their deep wells, moments of such gratitude I can hardly express it. As authors, we need each other. We need each other's words, each other's medicine. We need each other's stories to give us the courage to tell our own, and to tell the truth of how we got here. Thank you to every author who inspired me.

The work of writing a book is very much a personal endeavor, until it isn't. I write in a bubble, an incubator where the words flow, where I challenge my own assumptions, where I show up and ask if I can offer some sort of healing to the people who will read my words. And then I hand it off to my team and work alongside the people who choose to believe in those words.

To my agent, Rachelle, my speaking agent, Jim, and my team at Brazos: Thank you for taking my calls and responding to my emails, for believing in my words and encouraging me to remain true to who I am and what I hope to bring to the world. I'm grateful to have you as my community.

To my developmental editor, Rachel, and Julie, and the others who reviewed these pages: Led by the power of kinship and care, you helped me edit this book to make it stronger, thank you for showing up for me.

To Simran for writing a foreword that made me cry: Thank you for being my friend and for choosing to lean into stories of complexity and love.

To Soni: I dreamt of you designing the cover for this book long before you said yes, and I am so grateful for the way you infuse healing into the world through creativity. Thank you for listening to your own soul to give us art that so beautifully and tenderly reflects what this book is about.

To my sacred writing circles: Thank you for being in community with me.

To the Liminality Journal Community: You are some of my favorite people on the internet, and the way you show up for one another and for me is inspiring on a daily basis.

To those who gather with me for writing sessions every month: Thank you for holding space for me to write this book alongside you.

To Travis, Eliot, and Isaiah: Thank you for always, always supporting me, no matter what. You give me space when I need to write, you remind me that I'm doing a good job, you encourage me to rest when I need it most, and you show me what it means to laugh, adventure, and embrace the world around me with passion and care. Travis, you are my greatest adventure partner. Thank you for climbing with me when I need to get out of my head and for showing me what it means to celebrate joy and laughter in a hurting world. Thank you for helping me edit my way through last-minute panics when I doubted myself. The three of you make my life beautiful, and you inspire me to make the world a better place every single day.

To Blaze and Jupiter: Thank you for pulling me away from the computer a few times a day to remind me what it means to play, to eat a hearty snack, and to rest. You are my snuggliest companions, and I'm so grateful to have you in my life.

To all my ancestors and to future generations: I'm holding the space between you, and I hope that you feel ripples of healing in one way or another. Thank you for holding me steady and for reminding me through Mother Earth what it means to embody healing and care. You have helped me find my way again and again, and you help me tell a better story.

And to every person who picks up this book and decides to read it: Thank you for using your sacred imagination to go on this journey alongside me. We can heal on our own, but we cannot fully heal without one another. May we find ways, big and small, to heal the world—together.

NOTES

Foreword

1. Nicola Yoon, *Everything, Everything* (Ember, 2015), question and answer section, n.p.

Chapter 1 The Origins of Stories

1. Sam Coley, "Nature Now! Acorns: This Is Just Nutty," North Carolina Museum of Natural Sciences, April 20, 2021, https://naturalsciences.org/calendar/news/nature-now-acorns-this-is-just-nutty.

2. Kaitlin B. Curtice, *Living Resistance: An Indigenous Vision for Seeking Wholeness Every Day* (Brazos, 2023), 56.

Chapter 2 Oak Stories

1. Douglas W. Tallamy, *The Nature of Oaks: The Rich Ecology of Our Most Essential Native Trees* (Timber, 2021), 86.

2. Kevin Wilson, *The Way of Chai: Recipes for a Meaningful Life* (Tarcher Perigee, 2023), 37.

3. "History of Sherwood Forest, Robin Hood and Major Oak," Nottinghamshire City Council, February 10, 2025, https://www.nottinghamshire.gov.uk/culture-leisure/country-parks/history-of-sherwood-forest-robin-hood-and-major-oak.

4. James Godfrey-Faussett, "Oak Trees: Kings of Biodiversity," One Earth, May 30, 2024, https://www.oneearth.org/oak-trees-kings-of-biodiversity/.

5. Amber Morseau, "Learning Together by the Water," Maawndoonganan: Anishinaabe Resource Material to Accompany the State of Michigan Social Studies Standards, August 5, 2024, https://www.michigan.gov/mdcr/-/media/Project/Websites/mdcr/brochures/dei/Anishinaabe-Resource-Manual.pdf.

Chapter 3 Stories Are Mirrors

1. "What Is Hildegard's Viriditas?," Healthy Hildegard, accessed March 6, 2025, http://www.healthyhildegard.com/hildegards-viriditas.

Chapter 4 The Shape of Stories

1. Douglas W. Tallamy, *The Nature of Oaks: The Rich Ecology of Our Most Essential Native Trees* (Timber, 2021), 120.
2. AJ Eversole, "The Joy of Native Storytelling Structures," *We Need Diverse Books* (blog), December 10, 2020, https://diversebooks.org/joy-of-native-storytelling.
3. "Afghanistan: Taliban Deprive Women of Livelihoods, Identity," Human Rights Watch, January 18, 2022, https://www.hrw.org/news/2022/01/18/afghanistan-taliban-deprive-women-livelihoods-identity.

Chapter 5 Gathering Stories

1. Tommy Caldwell, *The Push: A Climber's Search for the Path* (Penguin, 2022), 235.
2. Jennie Egerdie, *Frog and Toad Are Doing Their Best: Bedtime Stories for Trying Times, A Parody* (Hachette Books, 2021), 30.
3. Rainesford Stauffer, *All the Gold Stars: Reimagining Ambition and the Ways We Strive* (Hachette Books, 2023), 27.

Chapter 6 Stories of Faith and Religion

1. Elise Loehnen, *On Our Best Behavior: The Seven Deadly Sins and the Price Women Pay to Be Good* (Dial, 2023), xviii.
2. Reza Aslan, *God: A Human History* (Random House, 2017), xiii.
3. Howard Thurman, *Jesus and the Disinherited* (Beacon, 1976), 2.
4. Eckhart Tolle, *A New Earth: Awakening to Your Life's Purpose* (Penguin Books, 2016), 70.
5. Douglas W. Tallamy, *The Nature of Oaks: The Rich Ecology of Our Most Essential Native Trees* (Timber, 2021), 11.

Chapter 7 Returning to Our Body's Stories

1. Elise Loehnen, *On Our Best Behavior: The Seven Deadly Sins and the Price Women Pay to Be Good* (Dial, 2023), 126.

Chapter 8 A Maze of Stories

1. David Brooks, *The Second Mountain: The Quest for a Moral Life* (Random House, 2019), 130.

Chapter 9 Stories of Aging and Happiness

1. Heather Corinna, *What Fresh Hell Is This? Perimenopause, Menopause, Other Indignities, and You* (Hachette Books, 2021), 7.
2. Sharon Blackie, *Hagitude: Reimagining the Second Half of Life* (New World Library, 2022), 3.
3. Leonie Hayden, "Decolonise Your Body! The Fascinating History of Māori and Periods," The Spinoff, April 17, 2019, https://thespinoff.co.nz/atea/17-04-2019/decolonising-your-body-maori-attitudes-to-periods.
4. Dan Buettner, *Live to 100: Secrets of the Blue Zones*, documentary series, Netflix, 2023.
5. "The Blue Zones Story," Blue Zones Project, March 9, 2025, https://info.bluezonesproject.com/origins.
6. Arthur C. Brooks and Oprah Winfrey, *Build the Life You Want: The Art and Science of Getting Happier* (Portfolio, 2023), 95–96.
7. Emily McGowan, "What Is a Third Place? (And Why You Should Have One)," The Good Trade, September 25, 2024, https://www.thegoodtrade.com/features/third-place-community-spaces.

Chapter 10 Stories We Tell About One Another

1. Alice Wong, *Year of the Tiger: An Activist's Life* (Knopf Doubleday, 2022), 268.
2. Kaitlin B. Curtice (@KaitlinCurtice), "To my Indigenous Kin," X (formerly Twitter), March 11, 2024, https://x.com/KaitlinCurtice/status/1767176206112235699.
3. Vandana Shiva, foreword to *Grandmothers' Wisdom* (Synergetic, 2024), 148.

Chapter 11 Stories of Myth and Othering

1. Joseph Campbell with Bill Moyers, *The Power of Myth* (Anchor Books/Doubleday, 1988), 206.
2. Clarissa Pinkola Estés, *Women Who Run with the Wolves: Myths and Stories of the Wild Woman Archetype* (Ballantine Books, 1996), 229.
3. John O'Connor, *The Secret History of Bigfoot: Field Notes on a North American Monster* (Source Books, 2024), 104.
4. Tom Ward, "When Edmund Hillary Went in Search of the Yeti," Atlas Obscura, February 15, 2022, https://www.atlasobscura.com/articles/edmund-hillary-yeti-hunt-nepal.

5. Dan Sasuweh Jones, *Living Ghosts and Mischievous Monsters: Chilling American Indian Stories* (Scholastic, 2021), viii.

6. O'Connor, *Secret History of Bigfoot,* 92.

7. Celeste Larsen, *Heal the Witch Wound: Reclaim Your Magic and Step into Your Power* (Weiser Books, 2023), 31.

8. Elise Loehnen, *On Our Best Behavior: The Seven Deadly Sins and the Price Women Pay to Be Good* (Dial, 2023), 15.

Chapter 12 Stories of Sports and Exploration

1. Chelsey Luger and Thosh Collins, *The Seven Circles: Indigenous Teachings for Living Well* (HarperOne, 2022), 33. Chelsey is a member of the Turtle Mountain Band of Chippewa and Standing Rock Sioux Tribe in North Dakota, and Thosh Collins is On Akimel O'odham, Seneca-Cayuga, and Osage.

2. *Home Game,* season 1, episode 1, "Calcio Storico," written by Ryan Duffy, directed by Austin Reza, aired June 26, 2020, on Netflix.

3. Naomi Osaka, "It's O.K. Not to Be O.K.," *Time,* July 8, 2021, https://time.com/6077128/naomi-osaka-essay-tokyo-olympics/.

4. Elise Loehnen, *On Our Best Behavior: The Seven Deadly Sins and the Price Women Pay to Be Good* (Dial, 2023), 23.

5. Brigid Delaney, "Forget the Bucket List, Forget the Ego: If You Want to Be a Hero, Stop Conquering Everest," *The Guardian,* September 1, 2016, https://www.theguardian.com/commentisfree/2016/sep/02/forget-the-bucket-list-forget-the-ego-if-you-want-to-be-a-hero-stop-conquering-things.

6. Luke Buckmaster, "Sherpa: Norbu Tenzing on the Everest 'Circus' and the Inevitability of Another Disaster," *The Guardian,* March 29, 2016, https://www.theguardian.com/film/2016/mar/30/sherpa-norbu-tenzing-on-the-everest-circus-and-the-inevitability-of-another-disaster.

7. Mariana Mendoza, "Grappling with Contradiction: Mariana Mendoza Moves to Decolonize Climbing," Center for Story-Based Strategy, October 28, 2019, https://www.storybasedstrategy.org/blog-full/2019/grappling-with-contradiction-mariana-mendoza.

8. Matt Samet, "First Look: Stone Locals—An Interview with Co-Director Mikey Schaefer," Climbing, August 26, 2020, https://www.climbing.com/news/first-look-stone-locals-an-interview-with-co-director-mikey-schaefer.

9. "Stone Locals: Rediscovering the Soul of Climbing," posted August 27, 2020, by Patagonia, YouTube, https://www.youtube.com/watch?v=Yj7ZCYMgSvw.

Chapter 13 Stories Are Labels

1. Rainer Maria Rilke, *Letters to a Young Poet* (Dover Publications, 2021), 45.

2. Kaitlin B. Curtice, *Native: Identity, Belonging, and Rediscovering God* (Brazos, 2020), 67.

3. Najwa Zebian, *The Only Constant: A Guide to Embracing Change and Leading an Authentic Life* (Harmony, 2024), 16.

4. Atlas Obscura editors, "Gordon Hirabayashi Campground," Atlas Obscura, September 16, 2021, https://www.atlasobscura.com/places/gordon-hirabayashi-campground.

5. Alex Hannold, host, *Climbing Gold*, podcast, "The Fighter," November 24, 2023, https://www.climbinggold.com/episodes/the-fighter.

6. Jose Antonio Vargas, *Dear America: Notes of an Undocumented Citizen* (Dey Street, 2018), 140–41.

Chapter 14 Stories of Land and Food

1. "Coldplay: The Moon Music Interview with Zane Lowe," posted September 30, 2024, Coldplay, YouTube, https://www.youtube.com/watch?app=desktop&v=6xt7nTuO85A.

2. Jennifer Grenz, *Medicine Wheel for the Planet: A Journey Toward Personal and Ecological Healing* (University of Minnesota Press, 2024), 55.

3. Michael Lee, "The Surprising Origins of the Fortune Cookie," History, February 11, 2021, https://www.history.com/news/fortune-cookies-invented-chinese-japanese.

4. Michael W. Twitty, *Koshersoul: The Faith and Food Journey of an African American Jew* (Amistad, 2022), 5.

5. Twitty, *Koshersoul*, 2.

6. Reem Kassis, *We Are Palestinian: A Celebration of Culture and Tradition* (Crocodile, 2023).

Chapter 15 Stories Told in Public

1. "News Platform Fact Sheet," Pew Research Center, September 17, 2024, https://www.pewresearch.org/journalism/fact-sheet/news-platform-fact-sheet/.

2. Africa Brooke, *The Third Perspective: Brave Expression in the Age of Intolerance* (Hachette Books, 2024), 63–64.

3. Heather Kelly, "From TV to TikTok: How We Get the News Is Changing Fast," *Washington Post*, November 15, 2023, https://www.washingtonpost.com/technology/2023/11/15/news-trends-social/.

4. Dorcas Cheng-Tozun, *Social Justice for the Sensitive Soul: How to Change the World in Quiet Ways* (Broadleaf Books, 2023), 70.

Chapter 16 Stories of Belief and Letting Go

1. John O'Connor, *The Secret History of Bigfoot: Field Notes on a North American Monster* (Source Books, 2024), 101–2.

2. Elizabeth Svoboda, "Why Is It So Hard to Change People's Minds?," *Greater Good Magazine*, June 27, 2017, https://greatergood.berkeley.edu/article/item/why_is_it_so_hard_to_change_peoples_minds.

3. Mark Nepo, *Surviving Storms: Finding the Strength to Meet Adversity* (St. Martin's Essentials, 2022), 70.

4. "Religious 'Nones' in America: Who They Are and What They Believe," Pew Research Center, January 24, 2024, https://www.pewresearch.org/religion/2024/01/24/religious-nones-in-america-who-they-are-and-what-they-believe/.

5. "Modeling the Future of Religion in America," Pew Research Center, September 13, 2022, https://www.pewresearch.org/religion/2022/09/13/modeling-the-future-of-religion-in-america/.

6. Kaitlin Curtice, "Mother-Earth-Driven Politics," *The Liminality Journal*, July 15, 2024, https://kaitlincurtice.substack.com/p/mother-earth-driven-politics.

7. Jeremy Seifert and Fred Bahnson, "The Forest Beyond," *Emergence Magazine*, April 20, 2023, https://emergencemagazine.org/film/the-forest-beyond/.

Chapter 17 Interfaith, Expansive, Futuristic Stories

1. Steven Charleston, *We Survived the End of the World: Lessons from Native America on Apocalypse and Hope* (Broadleaf Books, 2023), 19.

2. Keolu Fox, "A Future in Indigenous Hands," *National Geographic Indigenous Futures* 246, no. 1 (July 2024): 119.

3. Eboo Patel, *We Need to Build: Field Notes for Diverse Democracy* (Beacon, 2022), 13.

4. Sara Gurulé, "Tree Rings," The Coalition to Dismantle the Doctrine of Discovery, June 17, 2024, https://dismantlediscovery.org/2024/06/17/tree-rings/.

5. Kaitlin B. Curtice, *Living Resistance: An Indigenous Vision for Seeking Wholeness Every Day* (Brazos, 2023), 191.

6. James Vukelich, *The Seven Generations and the Seven Grandfather Teachings* (pub. by author, 2024).

Chapter 18 Merging Stories

1. Kaitlin Curtice, "Empathy," *The Liminality Journal*, May 4, 2024, https://kaitlincurtice.substack.com/p/day-4-empathy.

2. Kaitlin B. Curtice, *Living Resistance: An Indigenous Vision for Seeking Wholeness Every Day* (Brazos, 2023), 179.

3. Pooja Lakshmin, *Real Self-Care: A Transformative Program for Redefining Wellness* (Penguin Life, 2023), 61.

4. Rae Wynn-Grant, *Wild Life: Finding My Purpose in an Untamed World* (Zando, 2024), 52–53.

5. Prentis Hemphill, *What It Takes to Heal: How Transforming Ourselves Can Change the World* (Random House, 2024), 43.

6. Leah Lakshmi Piepzna-Samarasinha, *The Future Is Disabled: Prophecies, Love Notes, and Mourning Songs* (Arsenal Pulp, 2022), 29.

7. John Philip Newell, *Sacred Earth, Sacred Soul* (HarperOne, 2021), 67–68.

Chapter 19 Stories for Healing

1. *Doctor Who*, season 1, episode 8, "Empire of Death," written by Russell T. Davies, directed by Jamie Donoughue, aired June 21, 2024, on Disney+.

2. Alua Arthur, *Briefly Perfectly Human: Making an Authentic Life by Getting Real About the End* (Mariner Books, 2024), 15.

3. J.S. Park, *As Long as You Need: Permission to Grieve* (W Publishing, 2024), 22.

4. William Bryant Logan, *Oak: The Frame of Civilization* (Norton, 2005), 291.

5. "This Man Is Simply Beautiful," posted May 5, 2021, by Reflections on Life, YouTube, https://www.youtube.com/watch?v=mRF1GUZHDIo.

Chapter 20 The Future of Storytelling

1. Chris La Tray, *Becoming Little Shell: A Landless Indian's Journey Home* (Milkweed, 2024), 262.

2. Wayne K. Clatterbuck, "Tree Wounds: Response of Trees and What You Can Do," UT Extension, accessed March 6, 2025, https://utia.tennessee.edu/publications/wp-content/uploads/sites/269/2023/10/SP683.pdf.

3. *We Are Still Here: Afghan Women on Courage, Freedom, and the Fight to Be Heard* (Penguin, 2022), 132.

4. Howard Thurman, *Jesus and the Disinherited* (Beacon, 1976), 14.

5. Reza Aslan, *God: A Human History* (Random House, 2017), 169.

KAITLIN B. CURTICE is an award-winning author, poet-storyteller, and public speaker. As an enrolled citizen of the Potawatomi nation, she writes on the intersections of spirituality and identity and how they shift throughout our lives. She also speaks on these topics to diverse audiences who are interested in truth telling and healing. As an inter-spiritual advocate, Kaitlin participates in conversations on topics such as colonialism in faith communities, and she has spoken around the world on the importance of interfaith relationships. She has written online for *Sojourners*, Religion News Service, *On Being*, *SELF Magazine*, Oprah Daily, and more. Her work has been featured on CBS and in *USA Today*. She also writes at *The Liminality Journal*. Kaitlin lives in Philadelphia with her family.

CONNECT WITH KAITLIN

kaitlincurtice.com